HOW TO ESTABLISH

YOUR OWN

INDEPENDENT

PRIVATE PRACTICE

Fifth Edition

Donald E. Hendrickson, Ed.D.

James E. Fraze, CPA

68069

 **ACCELERATED DEVELOPMENT INC.**

Publishers

Muncie,   Indiana

HOW TO ESTABLISH YOUR OWN INDEPENDENT PRIVATE PRACTICE

Donald E. Hendrickson, Ed.D.
James E. Fraze, CPA

Library of Congress Catalog Number: 86-71219

International Standard Book Number: 0-915202-64-6

Printed in the United States of America

 ACCELERATED DEVELOPMENT Inc.
Publishers
3400 Kilgore Avenue, Muncie, IN 47304

68069

ACKNOWLEDGEMENTS

Many supportive individuals too numerous to mention have been consistently helpful and understanding in our endeavors to complete this manual.

We especially appreciate the kindness and patience of our wives, who have provided continuous support.

Gratitude is also expressed to those individuals who have attended our workshops, made helpful suggestions, and provided us with support and encouragement.

Donald E. Hendrickson
James E. Fraze

FORWARD

HOW TO READ THIS BOOK

To read and use this book with the greatest efficiency, follow these steps:

(1) Get a sense of the range of each topic by reading all the way through the text of one section. In this initial reading, ignore references to samples.

(2) Go back and review those subsections applicable to your particular practice. Then examine the samples (numbered and located for ease of reference at the end of each section) listed in the text.

(3) Since the concerns of an individual practice are **virtually identical** to those of a group practice, you need only determine the volume of your practice to tailor information to your own circumstances. Use **common sense** in scaling up and down information to meet your particular needs.

TABLE OF CONTENTS

TABLE OF CONTENTS

Section   **Pages**

INTRODUCTION

NOTES

INTRODUCTION

Designed to guide or at least to assist anyone who wants to learn how to establish a private practice (individual or group, part-time or full-time), this book is predicated upon the inescapable fact that a successful, healthy, stable private practice must have a sound financial base. The popular impression of the benefits of a private practice—large financial profit, prestige in the community, the promise of independence—often fails to weigh the burden of responsibilities which attend a private practice. One of our aims is to make practitioners aware of the obligations incurred in a private practice and, to that end, this book will be revealing, straightforward, and all-encompassing.

Should you make the decision to begin a private practice, you will need a great deal of advice about setting up an office, building a practice, creating an orderly paper flow, and operating according to the laws of the land. This book will serve as a ready reference tool for each of these procedures.

In private practice you must wear many hats: you will be a practitioner, a business executive, an employer, an investor, a clerical director, a strategist, and an authoritarian figure. To help you comprehend, control, and perform these roles, we have outlined readily-adaptable techniques and plans which have proven successful in a very large number of private practices.

The success or failure of a practice hinges upon the practitioner's knowledge of all options and obligations in the operation of that practice. To insure that successes will outnumber failures, we have offered approaches to various matters, ranging from scheduling appointments to fee-collecting, from insuring the premises to bookkeeping. **It is all here.**

The romantic notion that careful attention to financial concerns is somehow incompatible with the professional mission is not only misleading but potentially tragic, for no one can perform a professional service for very long if the income which sustains and supports that service is improperly or carelessly managed. We therefore strongly advise you to read and study every section in this book before making a major decision. **The methods herein are proven winners. We recommend them as the best examples of good professional practice and good business.**

NOTES

SECTION I

CONSIDERATIONS FOR A PRIVATE PRACTICE

NOTES

SECTION I
CONSIDERATIONS FOR A PRIVATE PRACTICE

Your **honest answers** to the following questions should provide the **information** you need to decide whether or not to establish a private practice.

I. In General

A. Do you **want** and **need** a private practice? Why?

B. Do you want a **full-time** or **part-time** practice? (How many days per week would constitute part-time?)

C. Are you capable of putting in the **long hours** it will take to establish your practice?

D. Are you capable of **successfully maintaining** your practice?

E. Can you work in a **private setting** for, or with, someone else?

F. Can you function as, and do the work of, an **administrator**?

G. Can you handle the **business** end (especially the *accounting* and *administrative*) of a private practice?

H. Do you have the **finances** for the initial investment or the means to obtain them?

II. In Particular

A. Are you a **self-starter** who gets work done without another's aid?

B. Do you have the **potential** to get along with a partner, staff, and patients?

C. Are you a good worker who assumes **responsibility**?

D. Do you have **leadership qualities** and the capacity to organize the operation to function at full potential?

E. Are you willing to **delegate authority** and responsibility? (Can you resist the impulse to do all the work yourself?)

F. Can you make a **decision** and stick to it?

G. Are you **healthy** and **energetic** enough to contribute your full resources to the practice?

III. In Regard to Finances

A. How much will you need for the **initial investment?**

B. Exactly how much **can you afford** to put into the business?

C. Have you discussed your financial situation with your **banker**?

D. Will you need financial assistance *in addition* to a bank loan?

E. Are you **eligible** for, and willing to consider, **other types** of financial assistance?

F. Have you calculated the difference between your **gross** and **net income** in the first year?

G. Can you **support yourself** (and your family) with the net income?

IV. In Partnership Or Corporation

A. Do you **want** and **need** a partner?

B. Do you have someone in mind who will work and do an **equal share,** whom you like and are able to get along with in critical situations?

C. Is this person **needed for** professional expertise, for business experience, or for financial assistance?

D. Have you carefully evaluated the **advantages** and **disadvantages** of both an individual practice and a partnership?

E. Should you **incorporate** your practice?

F. Some states restrict **professional incorporation** to individuals from the same profession. Does your state permit professional corporations? Are there certain restrictions?

G. Have you sought advice from an **accountant** and an **attorney** in regard to both partnership and incorporation?

V. About Your Practice

A. With how many professionals in private and clinic settings in your community will you **have to compete**?

B. In terms of the number of patients treated and the **potential net income,** how successful are these professionals? (Is your information accurate or guess work?)

C. Have you estimated how many people might **utilize** your service? Can you determine from which segment of the community these people will come?

D. Have you considered all options for a **referral system**? (Possibilities include social agencies, courts, mental health agencies, ministers, and physicians.)

E. Have you considered offering **special services** such as group work, marital therapy, TA, Gestalt, family therapy, psychological testing, biofeedback, or hypnotherapy?

SECTION II

CONSIDERATIONS BEFORE INITIATING

YOUR PRIVATE PRACTICE

NOTES

SECTION II
CONSIDERATIONS BEFORE INITIATING YOUR PRIVATE PRACTICE

Your consideration of all of the following items should provide **optimum preparation for the initiation of a private practice.**

I. Location

    A. The office should be **easy to find**, on or near familiar streets, close to bus lines, and as close as possible to the homes of prospective patients.

    B. The office should be **close to other** professional offices (medical, dental, social).

    C. **Adequate parking space** should be available, and both the building and the parking area should be lighted well enough to provide for the safety of the evening patients. (Good lighting is especially important when emergencies occur and when there is a regional time change.)

II. Building

    A. The building should be **attractive**—at least visually compatible with the image of a professional service—and should have the potential to meet future needs in the event that the patient load increases and you add staff members.

    B. The building should be in **good condition**. If some improvements are needed, make sure renovation will not require a large investment.

    C. You can **buy or lease.** If your lease, find out (1) if you have an option to renew or buy; (2) if the option contains a formula for determining the amount of rent for the renewal period; and (3) determine if an esculation clause is included to increase your monthly rent payments yearly (flat percent vs. cost of living).

    D. **Before signing a contract,** establish an agreement about repairs. (Is the responsibility for repairs yours or the owner's?) Also, determine who is responsible for insurance, property taxes, utilities, custodial service, maintenance supplies, etc.

    E. **Review** the terms of **sale** or the **lease** and the zoning regulations with an attorney.

III. Equipment and Office Supplies

    A. You will need **new** and/or **used** furniture (desk, desk chair, easy chair, end tables, lamps) and equipment (typewriter, file cabinet). Used items, if presentable, are appropriate. Special furniture and equipment needs of the administrative office, waiting room, therapy rooms, and your private office must also be assessed.

    B. A **copy machine** is an item you may wish to purchase or rent once your practice is fairly well established. Before making an investment, however, carefully weigh the the assets against the costs. Supplies (paper, ink) and maintenance (often available on a contractual basis) can be expensive.

    C. You will need **office supplies** (stationary, envelopes, stamps, typewriter ribbons, billing sheets, checks, accounting materials) and **professional supplies** (therapy forms, books, and perhaps a tape recorder, tapes, biofeedback apparatus).

D. You will need **miscellaneous supplies** (light bulbs, coffeemaker, coffee, filters, cups, kleenex, paper towels, toilet paper, aspirin). Added to the cost of periodic carpet cleaning, for example, the cost of these small items tends to add up to a large expense.

IV. **Professional Charges**

A. Contact the **state association** to see if there has been a recent survey concerning fees, or inquire about fees charged by other professionals in private practice in your area. Set comparable rates for your own services, taking into consideration whether or not these other professionals are part-time or full-time and whether or not their overhead is higher or lower than yours.

B. **Establish rates** for individuals and couples; for families and groups; and for other services such as biofeedback and psychological testing. You should also decide upon an hourly rate as well as a half hour rate for your therapy sessions.

C. Establish a **billing procedure** (options include monthly, weekly, semi-weekly, and by last name) and a policy about what percentage of the billed charges should be collected weekly or monthly and how much should be accumulated in accounts receivable.

D. **Determine** whether or not you can bill for third party insurance. If so, establish a method which includes a means to determine your eligibility.

E. Establish a **policy** for dealing with patients who encounter difficulty in paying bills. If you consider referral to a not-for-profit health agency, determine the extent and limitations of your obligation to a patient once the helping process has been initiated.

F. Contact a **collection agency** that charges reasonable rates, and establish a time period after which an unpaid account will be automatically turned over to the agency. (Unfortunately, the problem of unpaid bills is inevitable and persistent.) You should also establish a time period after which bad debts will no longer be kept on the books.

V. **Business Records**

A. Contact a **qualified accountant** to assist you in the preparation of your business records and to help you in obtaining your Federal I.D. number, establishing checking accounts and an accounting system for proper and accurate record-keeping.

B. Establish a **record system**, including a billing form and control sheet, for each patient contact. If you have a professional staff, provide forms on which they can log their patient contacts and services rendered.

C. Make copies of **all** insurance forms submitted so that proper follow-up billing is insured.

D. Make the keeping of payroll records as well as the recording of federal tax deposits, tax reports and payments a **regular part** of your business procedure.

E. Establish a method of **inventory-control** for general office supplies (stamps, envelopes, tapes, etc.).

F. Establish a block of time to **interpret** the monthly financial statement and to **project** for future months.

VI. **Professional Records**

A. You will need **Intake Forms** to establish each patient's identity, address, age, social security number, and insurance benefits.

B. You will need **Treatment Forms** to record each patient contact and a brief summary of the session.

C. You will need the **Diagnostic and Statistical Manual (DSM III)** for diagnosis and prognosis for the purpose of third party payment.

D. You will need **Release of Information Forms** in order to obtain information from other professionals.

E. You may want **Termination Forms** for closing a file or terminating a patient.

F. You will need other forms (Social History Outline, Psychological Report) and **Appointment Cards.**

VII. **Legal Matters**

A. Make sure you are **legally qualified** to establish a private practice. Some states require a special permit or license in addition to a state professional license or certification.

B. Familiarize yourself with **special laws** (for example, those covering workmen's compensation).

C. Consult with your **attorney** and **accountant** for assistance and information about the legal aspect of your practice.

VIII. **Insurance Protection**

A. You will need **professional liability insurance** —enough to cover the maximum limit your state places on malpractice.

B. You may need **liability insurance** should someone sustain an injury on your property.

C. You may need **fire insurance.**

D. You may want to establish a **pension plan** as well as **health, life** and **disability insurance** for yourself and your employees.

E. You may want to have an **alarm system** installed to protect against theft of equipment and private files.

SECTION III

ONE-PERSON HOME OFFICE

NOTES

SECTION III
ONE-PERSON HOME OFFICE

Home Office

I. Home Location and Zoning Laws

A. Familiarize yourself with local **zoning laws** concerning a home office.

B. Should the zoning laws be unfavorable, **contact a lawyer** to procure a **zoning variance.** To support the variance, contact residents within a two-block radius, inform them about the practice (times and length of business hours, maximum number of cars to be present at any given time), and get their signatures on a petition to approve the variance. (The petition should stipulate approval only for your practice—in case you vacate or sell.)

II. Parking and Office Entrance

A. There should be parking **adequate** for you, your family or staff, and for additional vehicles—either in the driveway, on the street, or in another area.

B. It is best to have a main entrance exclusively for patients. It will serve to **separate your practice from your personal life** and to eliminate contact between your family or staff and your patients, some of whom may be diagnosed as antisocial, paranoid, suspicious, or psychotic. If your home or office does not already have an entrance that can be used as a main entrance, or if it has one that could be used as such, you should consider building or modifying as long as no financial burden and no building or property depreciation result.

III. Physical Facilities

A. If your office facilities are inadequate, you should consider **modifications.** (Again, modifications should not result in a financial burden or property depreciation.)

B. **Lighting** should be installed on the outside of the building, on the main entrance (if you have one), and on the sidewalks to protect patients from accidents, attack, and robbery.

C. The facility should have a waiting room large enough to comfortably seat at least six people. (Family members or friends may accompany the patient being seen as well as the one waiting to be seen next.) **Inadequate waiting facilities inevitably produce confusion and distraction.**

D. The facility should be **soundproof** and equipped with adequate heating, lighting, and air-conditioning.

E. The facility should be equipped with a restroom, clothes rack or hooks, carpeting, ashtrays, and other accessories to **provide comfort.** (The restroom will eliminate patients' entering your private or home restroom.) In addition, a waiting room containing reading material of general interest, soft music of an non-monotonous sort, and a small aquarium will help patients to relax as they wait.

F. If you intend your practice to **encompass more** than individual therapy, your office should be large enough to also accommodate psychological testing, family therapy, and group therapy.

H. **Consider** equipping the facility with **an additional** (or multi-purpose) **office**— either for another therapist whom you might take into the practice to provide yourself with additional income, for use in separating family members with whom you wish to meet individually, for the maintenance of files, or for a secretary.

IV. **Secretary, Answering Service, Page and Pager, Self-Operation**

A. It is **best** to employ a secretary during your working hours to answer the phone, schedule and bill patients, type letters, and keep the books.

B. You should contract with an **answering service** to take care of calls when you are in session or when the secretary is unavailable. A 24-hour service is preferable to a telephone tape-recorder system which automatically records messages, not only because most people resent having to respond to a taped voice, but also because an answering service operator can provide callers with information as well as reassurance that you will call back shortly. Moreover, the operator can distinguish between emergencies and non-emergencies and can answer practical questions about office hours, etc. If an answering service is not available in your area, then you should purchase a telephone tape-recorder system which will automatically record all incoming messages.

C. A **pager** is an integral part of a successfully functioning practice. A pager is the link between you and your answering service, your office, and your home. When a call comes into one of these places while you are somewhere else, you can be reached within seconds. For example, upon receipt of a patient's call, the answering service operator calls the number assigned to the pager, who in turn sends out an electronic signal, which activates a receiver on your pager. You then call your answering service, get the patient's message, and return his or her call. This system provides you with mobility and virtually does away with worry about not being accessible to potentially suicidal patients.

A **pager** is an electronic signaling device which can be purchased or leased from either an answering service, the telephone company, or a manufacturer. Pagers are of four types: (1) the single-signal pager emits a beep or tone which alerts you to call your answering service; (2) the dual-signal pager emits two sounds, one clearly different from the other—allowing you to receive signals from, and simultaneously distinguish between, two different sources (for example, one sound—a pulsating beep—might be designated as the "call your office" signal, whereas the other sound—a steady tone—might mean "call your home"); (3) the voice pager allows the page (or any other sender) to transmit a spoken message to you (but you cannot transmit messages; and (4) the computer pager has a memory which will allow more than one call to be placed in a memory bank and be displayed on a small screen for the therapist. Both the single-signal pager and the dual-signal pager can be equipped with a silent (vibration and light) signal which you can receive while you are in a movie theater, in a meeting, or at a restaurant—a signal that no one else will be disturbed by. Communication range, which varies from pager to pager and from area to area, is available from the sales representative.

D. If **you choose not** to employ a secretary in your practice, then take about five minutes at the end of every session to: (1) reschedule the patient for the next appointment; (2) collect the charges; (3) stamp the check "for deposit only"; and (4) enter the appropriate information and the amount into the accounting book. Afterwards, take five or ten minutes to either write case notes or dictate them into a tape recorder. In the latter case, the tape can be dropped off or given to a typist who, after putting the notes on paper, can drop them by the office, where they can be placed in the patient files.

V. **Furniture, Equipment and Office Supplies**

    A. In a **one-person home office** the furniture for the therapy office as well as the waiting area may be already fully equipped, especially the waiting area, since it is probably the living room or family room of the family residence. This will help keep the total expense of opening an office down to a minimum amount.

    B. The **equipment** and **supplies** will probably need to be purchased since it is unlikely that they would be part of the household inventory.

    C. An **inventory sheet** is provided on the next page in order to give a breakdown of potential furniture, equipment and office supplies which might be needed **to open a one-person home office. Sample 1, pages 22-23.**

SAMPLE 1

ONE-PERSON HOME OFFICE

The **furniture, equipment** and **supplies** are listed below for the professional who plans to use one room of the home as the office and the family or living room as the waiting room. It is assumed that there will be no expense for the waiting room and/or receptionist area. Furthermore, for the purpose of this example it will be assumed that the private office has to be completely equipped.

GENERAL

Telephone hookups	$120.00
Telephone service monthly plus Yellow page ad	50.00
Insurance (fire, theft, liability in addition to home protection) per year	150.00
Insurance for malpractice ($100,000.00) per year	60.00
Newspaper advertising (Professional announcement)	400.00
Sub Total	$780.00

PROFESSIONAL OFFICE

1 Executive desk	274.00
1 Desk chair	194.00
1 Setee	175.00
2 Chairs @ $100.00	200.00
1 Set of book shelves	34.00
1 Cupboard	35.00
1 4 door file	114.00
1 Set of pictures	129.00
1 Desk lamp	30.00
1 Floor lamp	69.00
1 Typewriter table	44.00
Sub Total	$1,298.00

EQUIPMENT

1 Typewriter (used)	250.00
1 Clock	35.00
1 File sorter	9.00
1 Set of letter trays	15.00
1 Stapler	13.00
1 Tape dispenser	7.00
1 Pencil sharpener	12.00
5 Rubber stamps	26.00
1 Answering service (cassette tape answering machine)	239.00
1 Rolodex	24.00
3 pair book ends @ $2.00 ea.	6.00
1 Tape recorder	49.00
1 Wastebasket	3.00
Sub Total	$688.00

SUPPLIES

4 dozen pencils @ 1.00 ea.	4.00
1 paper punch	5.00
2 dozen 8½ x 11 pads @ 7.00 ea.	14.00
1 3M tape	1.00
1 box paper clips	2.00
1 pad phone messages	3.00
1 package purchase orders	5.00
3 ream Memo paper	14.00
1 box carbon paper	6.00
1 box typewriter paper	11.00
1 box 2nd sheet paper	10.00
2 hanging frames @ $5.00 ea.	8.00
6 boxes hanging folders @ $11.00 ea.	66.00
1 appointment book	9.00
1 doodle pad	5.00
1 box clasp envelopes	11.00
1 financial system	14.00
Supply of tests	130.00
Postage	34.00
Stationary 500	20.00
Envelopes 500	24.00
Announcements 200	36.00
Thank you for referrals cards 100	28.00
Business cards 500	17.00
Appointment cards 500	17.00
Sub Total	$494.00
Total	$3,260.00

On going **monthly expenses** to be considered for home office would include:

(1)	Telephone service plus long distance calls	$50.00
(2)	Telephone answering service if appropriate*	40.00
(3)	Postage	20.00
(4)	Insurance (on a monthly payment schedule)	15.00
(5)	Monthly payments on any furniture, equipment or supplies (rental or purchase).	?
(6)	Monthly payment to the bank for the loan to initiate the practice.	?
(7)	Payroll taxes and fringes if any	?
(8)	Legal and accounting	?
(9)	Dues and subscriptions	?
		?

*This will not be a monthly expense if a cassette tape answering machine is purchased.

NOTES

SECTION IV

ONE-PERSON OFFICE

OR

SMALL GROUP PRACTICE

IN A PROFESSIONAL BUILDING

NOTES

SECTION IV

ONE-PERSON OFFICE OR SMALL GROUP PRACTICE IN A PROFESSIONAL BUILDING

I. Location and Zoning Laws

A. The building should be **accessible to patients**, close to the offices of other professionals, and in close proximity to parking areas.

B. The building should be in an area **zoned** for private practice.

II. Physical Facilities

A. A one-person office should possess the **potential for expansion** should you decide at a later date to employ additional staff members or take in partners and create a professional partnership or corporation.

B. The facility should have a suitable waiting room, at least one office large enough to accommodate both individual and group consultation, at least one restroom (although two restrooms—one attached to the waiting room for patients, the other in the private area for staff—are preferable), and a kitchenette or counter area in another room where coffee can be made and which can serve as a retreat from the office-and-waiting-room area.

C. An office with a back door is generally preferable to one with a single entrance through which everyone must pass. The back door can be a convenient "escape hatch" should you prefer to avoid patients' observing you when you have to walk in late for an appointment or leave between appointments to run an errand or take care of an emergency situation. Also, the back door makes it possible for family, relatives, and friends to enter and leave inconspicuously.

D. An office adjacent to other offices is generally preferable to one not in proximity to other office space. In the event that you decide to expand your practice, it may be possible to rent or lease adjacent office space and to connect it to your present facility with a doorway or walkway.

E. If you are inclined to have a larger practice sometime in the future, sign a one-year or no date lease rather than a long term lease, especially if the present facility does not have the potential to be expanded.

III. Secretary and Answering Service

A. It is best to employ a secretary on a full-time basis. However, a viable alternative is to hire a secretary who can be available during working hours or on a part-time basis (20 hours/week). The presence of a secretary in the office, especially during evening hours, serves as potential protection should you be held liable for anything occurring during a therapy session.

B. You should contract with an answering service to take care of calls when you are in session or when the secretary is unavailable. A **24-hour service** (described in One-Person Home Office Section IV B) **is preferable.**

V. Furniture, Equipment and Office Supplies

A. In a one-person or small group office there is a need to completely furnish the waiting/reception area, private offices and any other rooms which might be available in your location. If the office is properly equipped, then it will have a **professional appearance** as well as being very functional.

B. An **inventory sheet** is provided on the next page in order to give a breakdown of all furniture, equipment and office supplies which might be needed to open a one-person or small group practice. **Sample 2, pages 29-31.**

SAMPLE 2

ONE-PERSON OFFICE OR SMALL GROUP PRACTICE IN A PROFESSIONAL BUILDING

The furniture, equipment and supplies are listed below as a sample of what might be purchased in order to initiate a one-person office or small group practice. Any of the items could be purchased as new merchandise or used if appropriate—also, certain items could be purchased at a later date (such as the furniture for the second professional office). In some cases furniture from your home might be utilized on a temporary basis until you have established your practice.

OFFICE SETUP EXPENSES FOR TWO PROFESSIONAL OFFICES PLUS WAITING ROOM AND RECEPTIONIST AREA

Rent deposit	$200.00
Monthly rent	275.00
Electric bill monthly	50.00
Gas heat bill monthly	50.00
Janitor bill monthly	25.00
Telephone hookup	120.00
Telephone service monthly for 3 phones plus classified ads	60.00
Insurance (fire, theft, lability) per year	150.00
Insurance, Malpractice ($100,000.00) per year	60.00
Newspaper advertising	400.00
Sub Total	$1,390.00

FURNITURE FOR RECEPTIONIST OFFICE AND WAITING ROOM

6 chairs @ $30.00	180.00
1 corner table	40.00
1 end table	40.00
1 coffee table	60.00
1 desk	30.00
1 steno chair	109.00
1 4 drawer file	114.00
1 storage cupboard	129.00
1 set pictures	129.00
1 coat rack	29.00
1 floor lamp	69.00
1 table lamp	39.00
1 typewriter table	44.00
Sub Total	$1,012.00

FURNITURE FOR PROFESSIONAL OFFICES

2 executive desks @ $274.50	549.00
2 desk chairs @ $194.50	389.00
2 setee @ $175.00	350.00
2 chairs @ $100.00	200.00
2 set bookshelves @ $34.00	68.00
2 cupboards @ $35.00	70.00
Sub Total	$1,626.00

EQUIPMENT FOR OFFICES AND RECEPTION AREA

1 clock	35.00
1 file sorter	9.00
1 set letter trays	15.00
1 stapler	13.00
1 tape dispenser	7.00
1 pencil sharpener	12.00
5 rubber stamps	26.00
1 typewriter	250.00
1 answering service (cassette tape answering machine)	239.00
1 rolodex	24.00
6 pairs of book ends @ $3.00 ea.	18.00
2 tape recorders @ $49.00 ea.	98.00
2 wastebaskets @ $4.00	8.00
Sub Total	$754.00

SUPPLIES

4 dozen pencils @ 1.00 ea.	4.00
1 paper punch	5.00
2 doz. 8½ x 11 pads @ 7.00 ea.	14.00
1 tape	1.00
1 box paper clips	2.00
1 pad phone message	3.00
1 package purchase orders	5.00
3 reams memo paper @ 5.00 ea.	15.00
1 box carbon paper	6.00
1 box typewriter paper	11.00
1 box 2nd sheet paper	11.00
2 hanging frames @ $4.50 ea.	9.00
6 boxes hanging folders @ 11.00 ea.	66.00
1 appointment book	9.00
1 doodle pad	5.00
1 box clasp envelopes	11.00
4 8-track tapes @ 8.00 ea.	32.00
1 financial system	14.00
Supply of tests	130.00
Postage	34.00
Stationary 500	20.00
Envelopes 500	24.00
Announcements 200	36.00
Thank you for referrals 100	28.00
Business cards 500	17.00
Appointment cards 500	17.00
Sub Total	$529.00
Total	$5,311.00

On-going monthly expenses to be considered for this particular office would include:

(1)	Rent, utilities and janitor services	$400.00
(2)	Telephone service plus long distance calls	50.00
(3)	Telephone answering service if appropriate*	40.00
(4)	Postage	10.00
(5)	Insurance (on a monthly payment schedule)	12.50
(6)	Monthly payments on any furniture, equipment or supplies (rental or purchase)	?
(7)	Monthly payment to the bank for the loan to initiate the practice	?
(8)	Payroll taxes and fringes	?
(9)	Legal and accounting	?
(10)	Dues and subscriptions	?
		?

*A cassette tape answering machine was listed as an initial expense.

NOTES

SECTION V

INITIATING YOUR PRIVATE PRACTICE

NOTES

SECTION V
INITIATING YOUR PRIVATE PRACTICE

After obtaining professional office space and appropriate parking space, you still need to consider all of the following items before you open your doors to the public.

I. The Office—Individual, Small Group or Large Group Practice

A. The *waiting room* should contain five to seven seats (more seats for a large group practice), arranged to provide comfort and a pleasant atmosphere for patients. Magazines, toys, a coat rack, and a soft drink machine can be included. Other accessories to consider are audio speakers (for relaxing music), soft lighting, and a reception window with a sign asking each patient to report to the secretary-receptionist.

B. The **secretarial area** should be equipped with a secretary-receptionist's chair and large desk (with typing area) and with another desk for the billing clerk and/or part-time secretary (the second secretary or billing clerk is only necessary for a large group practice). The receptionist and the billing clerk should have separate telephones, and each should have his or her own typewriter and adding machine. Additional equipment includes files, storage cabinets, dictating machine, copy machine, clock, mail box with separate slots for each professional, cash box, scheduling calendar, wastebaskets, billing forms and box, letterhead stationary, envelopes, stamps, carbon paper, stapler, tape dispenser, etc.

C. The **administrative director's office** (if you are involved in a large group practice) should be equipped with an executive desk and chair, telephone, dictaphone, and a fireproof file to protect valuable records (billing sheets, checkbooks, accounting books, etc.). At least two comfortable chairs and an end table should be located across from the desk. Soft lighting, audio speakers, and wall hangings are appropriate. Paneled, painted, or wallpapered walls and a thick carpet will contribute positively to appearance and soundproofing.

D. **Individual therapy room(s)** should be large enough to contain a work area and a separate therapy area. The work area (which might include a desk, file cabinet, phone, dictating machine, bookcase, typewriter, and perhaps a clothes closet) should be out of the way or in one corner so that it does not intrude upon the therapy area, which should contain furniture similar to that found in a family room.

E. The **multi-purpose room** should be large enough to hold all the personnel at once — for meetings with staff, group therapy, family therapy, workshops for patients or professionals, and other kinds of consultation. Especially appropriate for eliminating the closed-in feeling a patient might experience in an individual therapy room, this room should also contain furniture similar to that found in a family room. This type of room is extremely helpful for a one-person office or a small/large group practice.

F. The **relaxation and biofeedback room** should be equipped with the specialized equipment that best suits its purposes. It should contain a reclining chair and, like all other offices, soft lighting and carpeting for soundproofing.

G. A **kitchen or staff lounge** is not a necessity, but can contribute significantly to the operation of the practice as an area of relaxation where you, your staff, and patients can get coffee. This area should be equipped with cabinets, a refrigerator, a sink, and a coffeemaker. A door to the outside to serve as a private entrance and exit is desirable.

H. Separate **restroom facilities** for both patients and professional staff should be available and stocked with appropriate supplies.

II. Professional Announcements

A. A newspaper ad should appear just prior to the opening of your office. So that the announcement is suitably professional, consult your professional code of ethics for specific criteria. (Before placing the ad, you should estimate the ad's size, the number of words it will contain, and the length of time you want it to run.) **Sample 3, page 39.**

B. Announcements may also be sent to other professionals in your community and to those nearby. These announcements should also conform to the criteria set forth in the code of ethics. Along with the announcement card a letter can be sent which gives a detail description of the individual, the practice and any area of expertise. **Sample 4, and 6 page 40-41.**

C. In the event that you relocate your practice, you have the responsibility to send out a simple announcement to the patients. **Sample 5, page 40.**

III. Telephone Directory Listing

A. An ad should be placed in the telephone directory. Since the directory is published only once a year in smaller cities (twice a year in some larger cities), you should contact the telephone company well before you intend to open your doors to the public. Again, the ad should conform to the code of ethics.

B. The ad can appear with name only under Physicians, Psychologists, Social Workers, Clinics, or Counselors. Another (larger) ad with an explanation of services offered can appear under Marriage and Family Counseling or Clinics. **Sample 7, page 42.**

IV. Telephone Answering Service

A. The answering service, which will answer the number listed in the telephone book and the one which appears on the appointment card and letterhead, should provide coverage for after hours and on weekends. Answering services are generally inexpensive, reliable, and professional in answering calls and accepting messages.

B. The answering service should be informed in writing as to how you want your calls handled. Your philosophy may differ significantly from that of other professionals who utilize the service. **Sample 8, pages 43-44.**

V. Telephone and Dictaphone

A. Extra telephone lines (or call waiting) should be installed according to needs of your practice. Patients will call to make, change, and cancel appointments; other professionals will make referral calls, and you will probably make several calls each day.

B. A dictating machine, which can be installed on the last line of your telephone, is a great convenience for in-office dictation. It should also have the capacity to receive incoming calls so that you can dictate messages from other locations, such as dictating letters, psychological reports or changes in your schedule from your home or several hundred miles away.

VI. Personnel

A. In employing an adequate office and professional staff, you must decide exactly what duties you want each individual to perform. Consider the overall personnel program: employee selection, the communication process, publication of personnel policies, terms of employment, salary and wages, employee benefits, in-service training, promotion, leaves, salary and wage administration, health and safety of employees, working conditions, employee facilities, complaint procedures, and the discipline of employees. **Sample 9, page 45-53.**

B. Each prospective employee should be required to complete an application for employment so that you will receive up-to-date information about his or her past employment record and be able to check with former employees and references. **Sample 10, pages 54-56.**

C. If you hire office and professional staff, a confidential wage/salary history of each employee should be maintained. **Sample 11, page 57.**

D. A record of each employee's work attendance should be maintained, especially because misunderstandings between employees and employers generally occur over such matters as sick days, special business days, professional training days, and vacation days. **Sample 12, page 58.**

E. The secretary-receptionist, employed to do the general office work, must also handle the billing if a billing clerk is not employed.

F. The duties of the secretary or receptionist are to collect fees paid during working hours, to answer all in-coming calls in a cheerful and courteous manner, to take messages, to refer calls to the proper persons, to schedule appointments, and to respect the confidentiality of information pertaining to the employer's business. Because the use of the telephone is so important to the practice, restrictions regarding personal use must be announced and enforced.

The secretary is further responsible for office filing. Should the secretary remove a bill or file from the card holder or cabinet, it is his or her responsibility to promptly and properly replace the material according to alphabetical order once it has been used. The secretary must also maintain a list (to be submitted to you or to your administrative director each week) of all patients who are not covered by insurance and who are delinquent in payment as well as a list of all patients who are covered by insurance. When payment is due for services rendered to such patients, the secretary must notify the billing clerk; also, the secretary should periodically check patient files to ascertain that insurance forms are present and properly signed.

G. The duties of the billing clerk are to handle all billing through the mail, including billing for insured patients; to promptly and properly replace bills or files in the card holder or cabinet according to alphabetical order once they have been used; to respect the confidentiality of information pertaining to the employer's business; to limit his or her use of the telephone according to the announced restrictions; to learn the duties and functions of the other secretaries; and to cooperate with other personnel.

It is the billing clerk's duty to keep the billing current. Bills must be processed and mailed at least every thirty (30) days, with the exception of bills to insurance companies which request alternate billing periods. In regard to such companies, billing is to be made as requested as long as the patient is being treated on a regular basis. However, if the patient is being treated on an irregular basis, billing is to be processed and mailed after each treatment.

It is the billing clerk's responsibility to bill all insurance carriers (including Blue-Cross, Medicaid, Medicare, the Veterans Administration) and self-pay patients on a weekly basis, for other professionals as well as hospitals bill against insurnce policies —and some policies are limited as to what kind of services and how many professionals per day can be reimbursed.

The billing clerk must inform the receptionist on a daily basis as to which patients need to provide or sign insurance forms. Also, when the billing clerk is working on bills, which are to be kept in card holders at all other times, he or she must keep the bills in one place and must never leave them in a desk drawer.

H. If one or more full-time professionals are to be employed, then it is necessary to have a mutual understanding from the beginning concerning time involvement, patient contact, vacation time, sick time, and professional training time and to sign a contract of agreement. Consult an attorney for a contract agreement. **Sample 13, pages 59-61.**

I. Consulting or part-time professional staff members must also sign a contract concerning time involvement, patient contact, etc. However, part-time professional staff members normally are not entitled to paid holidays, paid vacations, or paid sick leave. Consult an attorney for a contract agreement. **Sample 13, pages 59-61.**

J. Any time that you employ several individuals, there are certain federal regulations that must be adhered to, such as those set forth in the Fair Labor Standards Act, Title VII of the Civil Rights Act, the Age Discrimination Act, the Employee Retirement Income Security Act, and the Occupational Safety and Health Act. **Sample 14, pages 62-68.**

K. Because an employer is responsible for social security taxes, unemployment taxes, and workman's compensation insurance, you should become knowledgeable about what constitutes an employee and what constitutes an independent contractor. **Sample 64, pages 200-204.**

L. In order to determine if members of your staff are to be classified as employees or as independent contractors, you must complete an employment questionnaire for each person in your employ. This determination will aid you in making decisions about an insurance plan, retirement fund, FICA, FUTA, and income tax withholding for each prospective employee. **Sample 65, pages 205-206.**

SAMPLE 3

PROFESSIONAL ANNOUNCEMENT FOR NEWSPAPER

John Doe, Ph.D.
Psychologist

Diplomate in Counseling Psychology
American Board of Professional Psychology

Announced the Opening of his Office at

2801 Ethel Ave.
Suite 2
Corinthian Building
Muncie, Indiana 47304

Individual, Marital, Family and group Psychotherapy with
Children, Adolescents and Adults.
Hypnosis, and Biofeedback Treatment
Psychological and Educational Evaluations

By Appointment Only   **Phone 317/282-2863**

Consult the professional code of ethics for specific details as to how the ad should be displayed within a newspaper.

SAMPLE 4

PROFESSIONAL ANNOUNCEMENTS FOR MAILING TO PROFESSIONALS WITHIN THE COMMUNITY

JOHN DOE, PH.D.
Psychologist
Diplomate in Counseling Psychology
American Board of Professional Psychology

Announces The Opening of His Office
At
2810 Ethel Ave.
Suite 2
Corinthian Building
Muncie, Indiana 47304

Individual, Marital, Family and Group Psychotherapy
With Children, Adolescents and Adults.
Hypnosis and Biofeedback Treatment
Psychological and Educational Evaluations

By Appointment Only　　　　　　　　　**Phone 282-2863**

Consult the professional code of ethics for specific details concerning the professional announcement.

SAMPLE 5

ANNOUNCEMENT CARD SENT TO PATIENTS

Dear Patient:

John Doe, Ph.D. will be moving to
2810 Ethel Avenue, Suite 2
Corinthian Building, Muncie,
Indiana, 47304. We plan to move
June 16th. If you have any
questions do not hesitate to call us
at 282-2863.

Sample 6
LETTER OF INTRODUCTION

PSYCHOLOGISTS ASSOCIATES
John Doe, Ph.D.
PSYCHOLOGIST
DIPLOMATE IN COUNSELING PSYCHOLOGY, ABPP

Jane Doe, M.A.
THERAPIST

ANNOUNCEMENT

Dr. John Doe, formerly a partner of the Mutual Psychiatric Clinic, has recently opened his own private office. Dr. Doe has been active as a psychologist in private practice since 1972. He is certified by the State Board of Examiners in Psychology, member of several state and national professional associations including The American Psychological Association. Recently, he was awarded the Diplomate in Counseling Psychology by the American Board of Professional Psychology.

Dr. Doe can be reached for patient consultation or direct referral by calling or writing to:
2810 Ethel Avenue
Corinthian Bldg. Suite 2
Muncie, Indiana 47304
317/282-2863

24 HR. EMERGENCY SERVICE----------317/282-2863

Dr. Doe will provide individual, marital, family and group therapy with children, adolescents and adults. Additional services in the area of hypnosis, biofeedback, stress management and habit control are provided for the patients. Also, a full range of pyschological testing and a complete psychological evaluation can be requested by the referring physician or agency.

Treatment for patients includes, but is not limited to the following:

(1) Depression
(2) Adjustment problems
(3) Anxiety and poor stress tolerance
(4) Marital conflicts
(5) Family conflicts
(6) Problems of children and adolescents
(7) Alcohol and drug abuse
(8) Habit problems—weight and smoking
(9) Psychological, educational, court,
neurological and industrial evaluations
(10) Sexual difficulties
(11) Stress management for heart patients, high blood pressure
patients and other physical disorders
(12) Migraine and tension headaches
(13) Psychophysiological disorders
(14) Personality disorders

CALL 282-2863 FOR ADDITIONAL INFORMATION

SAMPLE 7

TELEPHONE LISTING FOR DIRECTORY

Marriage & Family Counselors

CATHOLIC CHARITIES OF THE MADISON
DIOCESE
Family Marital Counseling, and Child Welfare
1500 E. Jackson.......................286-4321
COUNTY PASTORAL COUNSELING
SERVICE
A Nationally Accredited Agency
Marital • Family • Group • Individual
716 W. 21st 257-1713

DOE, JOHN PH.D.

INDIVIDUAL, FAMILY, MARITAL
AND GROUP THERAPY
CHILDREN, ADOLESCENCE & ADULTS
HYPNOTHERAPY & BIOFEEDBACK
PSYCHIATRIC, PSYCHOLOGICAL &
EDUCATIONAL EVALUATIONS

2810 ETHEL AVE.
SUITE 2
CORINTHIAN BUILDING 282-2863

FAMILY COUNSELING SERVICE
Professional Help On Marriage, Family,
Personal, Parent-Child, Budget
Counseling—United Way Agency
Family Life Education
Family Service Assoc. Of America

Crisis Intervention Center 289-4141

615 Elm St..............................284-3161

HENRY, JOAN PH.D.
Individual & Family Therapy
325 S. 12..............................289-5167
MADISON PSYCHIATRIC CENTER
2915 S. Madison.......................286-1061
PSYCHIATRIC CLINICS, INC.
5502 W. University 289-2178
(See Advertistment This Classification)
SMITH, JOHN E. ACSW
Marriage and Sex Counseling
416 E. 5th.............................288-3411

PSYCHIATRIC
CLINICS, INC.

JOHN DOE, M.D.
PSYCHOLOGICAL TESTING & TREATMENT
GROUP—INDIVIDUAL—THERAPY
FAMILY—MARRIAGE—YOUTH
EVENING APPOINTMENTS AVAILABLE

289-2178
5502 W. University

An ad also can appear under the title of Clinics, Counselors, Physicians, Psychologists and Social Workers. This type of ad generally will only give the name of the clinic or professional person and the address and phone. The ad can also appear in the directory of surrounding communities. Consult the professional code of ethics for specific details concerning the advertising within the telephone directory.

SAMPLE 8

LETTER SENT TO ANSWERING SERVICE
PROVIDING INFORMATION CONCERNING
HOW REGULAR AND EMERGENCY
CALLS SHOULD BE HANDLED

PSYCHOLOGISTS ASSOCIATES
JOHN DOE, PH.D.
PSYCHOLOGIST
DIPLOMATE IN COUNSELING PSYCHOLOGY, ABPP

JANE DOE, M.A.
THERAPIST

Physicians Answering Service
100 South Main Street
National Bank Building
Muncie, Indiana 47305

Dear Mrs. Jones:

The following, I hope, will be of value to you and your staff.

When taking a call for me, please obtain the following information:

1. Patient's name and phone number.
2. A brief outline or idea of the problem so that it can be relayed to me, but do not push the caller if he or she does not wish to comply.

DO NOT REVEAL MY HOME PHONE NUMBER OR ADDRESS TO THE CALLER.

After obtaining the above information follow this procedure:

1. Call my page boy beeper—wait 15 minutes.
2. After 15 minutes then call my page boy beeper again—wait 15 minutes.
3. After a total of 30 minutes, then call my home.
4. If I am not at home, please contact any of the other therapist. If for any reason you are not able to reach the above mentioned persons, start down the list of therapists until you reach one at home; then explain the situation to that individual.

Dr. Donald Henry	Home 288-6442
Mr. Steve Keller	Home 288-8086
Dr. Barb Smith	Home 282-9613
Dr. Wayne Forrest	Home 288-8864
Dr. Steve Smith	Home 282-8068
Dr. June High	Home 282-4001
Dr. Jay Summer	Home 289-2241

2810 ETHEL AVENUE • SUITE 2 • CORINTHIAN BUILDING • MUNCIE, INDIANA 47304 • 317/282-2863

The list that you have dated May 17, 19____, is invalid and outdated. Please dispose of that list. If there are further changes, we will notify you.

Thank you for your assistance in this matter.

Sincerely yours,

John Doe, Ph.D.
Psychologist
Diplomate in Counseling Psychology, ABPP

SAMPLE 9

CONSIDERATION FOR PERSONNEL POLICY AND EMPLOYMENT

The following information has been adopted from literature developed by the Federal government and the government of the State of Indiana. This information is available free of charge from the Government Printing Office, Washington, D.C., and is produced for consumer use. The following passages have been modified in certain places to make the materials directly relevant to the topic at hand.

I. Overall Personnel Program

A. Does your personnel program effectively function in attracting, developing, maintaining and utilizing a stable, efficient and economical work force?

B. Does your statement of personnel policies define company objectives with respect to profitable operation, community and social responsibility and sound employee relations?

C. Does your personnel program serve to effectively communicate to employees the importance and relationship of their jobs to the overall operations of the company?

D. Is the responsibility for the proper formulation and administration of the personnel program clearly designated and delegated? Does the designee have the authority to properly carry out the function?

E. Is an employee recognized and treated as an individual or just a part of the group?

F. Is it an objective of your personnel program to make sure your firm is in compliance with all state and Federal laws and regulations? Is this responsibility clearly assigned to someone in your organization?

G. Is it an objective of your personnel program to respect the dignity of the individual employee and his or her right to privacy?

II. Employee Selection

A. Is a continuing effort made to fill job openings with qualified employees from within your operation? Do you make an effort to qualify those employees who are now with you for better jobs? By training? By instruction?

B. Are you missing a good source of steady employees by placing unnecessary or illegal restrictions on handicapped, female, minority or older person groups?

C. Do you utilize as sources of potential employees:

   Schools and colleges
   Private employment agencies
   State employment service
   Advertisements (radio, television, newspapers, etc.)
   Referrals
   Other sources (chambers of commerce, trade associations, etc.)
   Local, state, Federal training and vocational programs and agencies
   Social agencies

D. Are your hiring rates (including employee benefits) sufficiently competitive within your community so you can attract good people?

When was your last survey?

Do you know what your labor market competitors are offering their applicants?

E. Are you aware of the legal restrictions on the scope of the inquiries that may be made of a prospective employee?

Do you periodically update your interviewer(s) on changing laws and regulations in this area?

F. Do your application forms provide sufficient information on past work and education, history, personal and credit references, and career interests so that an employment risk will be readily apparent?

What do you really know about the people you employ?

How thorough are your reference checks?

Are these checks completed before applicants are placed on the job? If not, are they completed very soon thereafter?

Are all questions directly related to the individual's ability to do the job?

Have you reviewed your application form recently to make sure it is in compliance with local, state, and Federal civil rights laws?

G. Are the newly-hired people told what basic duties and responsibilities there will be?

Are their wage rate potential, "fringe" benefits, shifts, hours of work, plant and safety rules and regulations and other working conditions made clear before employment? How is this done?

Are they given a written explanation of benefits?

H. Do you have a follow-up orientation program with new employees 3 to 6 months after employment?

I. Do you use tests as part of the selection and placement process?

Do these tests result in disparate rejection rates of minorities or females?

Do you have sufficient data to support whether they do or not?

If your rejection rates seem to be disparate, have the tests been validated in terms of actual job performance and requirements?

If so, do they serve the function of establishing necessary qualifications?

Are your tests legal?

III. Communications

A. How much time and effort do you spend planning positive communications to your personnel?

Top management to supervisors?

Supervisors to employees?

B. What are your present forms of communication?

Are they effective?

Are you satisfied with them?

What do they communicate?

C. What is the upward communications climate in your operation?

Are you told just what your subordinate thinks you want to be told?

C. Have you surrounded yourself with "yes" people?

Have you established a climate that encourages forthright, upward communication?

Are there regular staff meetings to insure effective communication of relevant information to supervisors? If so, are the proper persons in attendance?

D. Are your supervisors and employees smothered with too much written communication? On the other hand, is there sufficient communication?

E. If you have an employee handbook, does it have eye appeal and explain your policies and benefits so they will be understood? Is it up to date?

F. Have you ever conducted an employee opinion and attitude survey in your operation?

Were the results communicated to your employees with some statement of your reaction and plan of action?

Did you effectuate your plan of action?

Did you follow up later to determine if any change occurred in employee attitude?

G. Do your employees participate in a suggestions system?

How many awards for suggestions have you made this year?

What is the quality of suggestions received?

Are the reasons for rejecting suggestions adequately explained to suggestors?

Are the program and the award winners receiving sufficient publicity?

H. Do you rely upon a "grapevine" and/or do you initiate communications to avoid the rumor mill?

I. Are your safety rules posted? Are they regularly updated?

J. Do you make use of exit interviews? Questionnaires to those who have terminated?

IV. **Publication Of Personnel Policies**

A. Have you clearly defined your personnel policies and procedures?

B. Are these policies and procedures consistent with Federal, state, and local laws and regulations (consider equal pay, age, wage and hour, equal employment opportunity, occupational safety and health)? Do you subscribe to a service or receive sufficient periodicals that continually update you on changes in legislation, court rulings and new concepts affecting personnel administration?

C. Do you review and update these policies and procedures on a regular basis? Are your management personnel and supervisors given an effective opportunity for input?

D. Are these updated policies and procedures clearly and effectively communicated to your supervisors and to your employees?

E. If you have an employee handbook for the purpose of communicating these policies and procedures to your employees, is it regularly reviewed and updated?

Are the revisions distributed to all employees so they have a complete updated handbook?

Is an effort made to determine that the handbook effectively communicates its contents to the employees?

F. Are these policies and procedures consistently enforced throughout your organization?

V. **Terms Of Employment**

Wages and Salaries

A. Are your wages and salaries in line with those paid by competitors in your labor market and do they reflect cost of living?

Do you have a good source for this information?

Reviewed periodically?

B. Do you have internal wage inequities?

Equal pay for equal work?

How do you know?

C. Do you regularly review your wage rates and employee performance with your employees? How? Are proper records kept?

Hours

A. Are your starting and ending times reasonable? Is consideration given to timing to avoid traffic congestion?

B. Do the working hours accomplish the dual purpose of meeting the needs of the company and suiting the convenience of the employee?

C. Are changes in work schedules and/or overtime requirements communicated sufficiently in advance of the need to work such hours?

D. Are your employees' work hours and overtime pay practices in line with your competition?

E. Does your operation meet all legal requirements for work by minors? (Work permits, hours, and hazardous occupations?)

F. Have you considered various scheduling techniques which will make your work schedules more attractive for the recruitment of higher caliber employees? (Flexible work week? 4-day work week? Flexible work day?)

G. Do your records accurately reflect actual hours worked?

Do they reflect days employee is off due to illness?

Will your records suffice for a wage-hour inspection?

Are hours worked for non-exempt personnel reported on pay check stub?

H. Have your efforts to comply with the overtime requirements of the Fair Labor Standards Act resulted in overburdening exempt employees by shifting work from non-exempt people?

I. Are job duties and salary tests of exempt employees reviewed periodically to insure compliance with Fair Labor Standards Act exempt status?

Other Employee Benefits

A. Is a sound group insurance (life, health, hospitalization, disability, or accidental death) plan available to employees?

A Health Maintenance Organization (HMO)?

Do you pay a fair share of the cost?

Do you have a current publication clearly explaining such benefits to your employees?

Does it explain the coordination of benefits clause in group health and accident policies?

Eligiblity requirements for various benefits?

B. You can save money through lower experience ratings under both unemployment and workmen's compensation programs. Who in your organization "rides herd" on these programs?

C. Are your employee benefits in line with your community competition? How do you reliably determine this?

D. Are benefits individually explained to new employees and changes carefully explained to all employees? By whom?

E. Are you aware of what percentage of your payroll dollars you spend on employee benefits? Are your employees?

F. Do you have a planned program for promoting the value of your benefits to your employees? Do they realize the advantage of the company providing the benefits over what it would cost them to secure the benefits themselves?

G. Do you know which benefits are most important to your employees so that you can secure the greatest value from your benefit dollars?

H. Are you meeting legal requirements in the administration of and reporting on your benefit programs?

I. What have you done to inform your employees' families of your benefit program?

J. Do you review administrative procedures to make certain that delays in processing employee claims are minimized and that there is no abuse of benefits by employees? Is eligibility clearly defined and established?

Training, Promotion, Placement, Leaves

A. Do all employees receive the kind of job instruction to enable them to do their job the best way?

   Does this include the safety and health aspects of the work?

   How is this accomplished?

B. Do your personnel records contain an education and skills inventory? Is it updated to reflect additional training?

C. Have jobs been studied recently to see if improvement can be made in terms of productivity and job enlargement or enrichment?

D. Do you have a policy on leave or time off to participate in governmental and civic affairs?

E. Do you have a consistent and well understood holiday pay eligibility policy?

F. Do you consistently require medical documentation for absences due to illness beyond a stated period of time?

G. Do you keep accurate records? Are attendance records reviewed periodically, especially for employees who are habitually absent on Mondays and Fridays or other patterns?

H. Do you have a written absenteeism policy which is understood by the employees? If so, are you specific about what is excusable?

   Is policy consistently enforced?

I. Is your maternity leave policy consistent with state and Federal laws, rules and regulations?

VI. Wage And Salary Administration

A. Do you have a qualified and experienced person assigned to the development and maintenance of wage and salary policies?

B. Do you pay properly for time spent in work activities of an unusual nature such as training, travel, employee meetings and the like?

C. Do you conduct audits periodically to insure compliance with wage-hour laws?

D. How frequently are your pay rates reviewed with your labor area rates?

Review of exempt salaries?

Review of benefits for comparable jobs and entry jobs?

E. Do you have a periodic review of employee performance?

Once a year, one every two years?

When?

Do employees understand it?

Are performance ratings tied to salary progression?

F. Do your supervisors understand the basic relationship between profits and ability to pay wages?

G. During the past year, what percentage of your employees have terminated due to unsatisfactory compensation?

VII. Health, Safety, Working Conditions, Employee Facilities

A. Is there someone in your organization who is responsible for a sound, well-developed safety program?

B. Do you have an active safety and health program to insure compliance with required Federal Occupational Safety and Health (OSHA) safety and health standards?

C. Have you ever considered asking your workman's compensation insurance carrier to assist you with a safety and health audit or self-inspection?

D. Have you posted in a conspicuous place the required safety and health poster from OSHA?

E. Is safety prompted through posters, safety talks, bulletins and employee training?

F. Have you documented all the things you have done (new equipment, training, safety procedures) in the safety and health area to demonstrate "good faith" to a government inspector?

G. Are there sufficient and well-maintained rest rooms and drinking water facilities?

H. Are your physical premises properly lighted, ventilated and heated?

   Noise level?

   Housekeeping?

I. Are your working conditions, building facilities and work areas as attractive as those of your competiton?

J. Are all exits properly marked? Sufficient number? Unobstructed?

K. Are periodic physical examinations required?

   Also pre-employment exams and/or health questionnaires?

   Exam on return from an illness or injury?

L. Are your safety rules clear, up-to-date and reasonable?

   Are they in writing?

   Do your employees know them?

   Posted?

   Are supervisors well-informed of the safety rules and procedures for handling violations of them?

M. Do you make an occasional practice of:

   Eating in your employee lunch room?

   Visiting break and recreation areas?

   Inspecting employee washroom?

   Touring your parking lot?

   Inspecting entire facility for safety and health practices?

N. Do employees participate in preventive maintenance and clean-up program?

O. Do you have established, well-known housekeeping standards?

VIII. **Complaint Procedure**

A. Do you have a formal or semi-formal procedure which allows employees to air complaints or problems?

   Is this procedure explained to employees periodically?

   Is it in writing and included in orientation and handout material?

Is there more than one step in this procedure from the immediate supervisor to those above?

B. Do you keep adequate records of complaints and how handled?

C. If there is no such formal procedure, to whom do employees turn when they feel they are not getting fair treatment?

D. Who is responsible for investigating complaints to determine if there are any deep-seated problems which should be remedied?

IX. Discipline Of Employees

A. Do employees know the company policies and rules, written or unwritten?

How are they informed? Posted?

B. Do you have and administer a consistent policy of discipline for employee misconduct? Reviewed and monitored to insure equal treatment?

C. Are disciplinary measures monitored to assure consistency and avoid disparate treatment?

D. Are all forms of discipline promptly made a matter of a well documented and comprehensive written record?

Where kept? How long?

E. Do you have a procedure for discharge? A witness?

F. Do you make certain any statements to the State Employment Security Division are consistent with statements to the employee?

SAMPLE 10

EMPLOYMENT APPLICATION FORM

APPLICATION FOR EMPLOYMENT
(Please Print Plainly)

Date:_____

PERSONAL

Name:_____S.S.#_____
      Last   First   Middle Initial

Present address: _____
          No.   Street   City   State   Zip

How long have you lived at this address?_____Telephone Number _____

Previous address: _____
             No.   Street   City   State   Zip

How long did you reside there?_____

How did you learn of this position?_____

Do you want to work_____full-time or_____part-time.

Specify days and hours if less than forty. _____

Have you been employed by us before?_____If so, when?_____

List any friends or relatives employed by us: _____

_____

If hired, on what date will you be available to start?_____

Are there any other experiences, skills, or qualifications which you feel would especially fit you for work with the Clinic?

If hired, do you have a reliable means of transportation to get to work? ____yes ____no

Do you have any physical handicaps which would prevent you from performing specific kinds of work?_____If yes, describe the defect(s) and explain the work limitations.

_____

_____

Have you had a serious sickness in the past four years?

_____No _____Yes (explain) _____

Have you ever received compensation for injuries?

_____No   _____Yes (explain) _____

Have you ever been convicted of a crime, excluding misdemeanors and traffic offenses?
_____No   _____Yes

If yes, describe in full _____

_____

_____

Person to be notified in case of accident or emergency:

Name: _____Phone Number:_____

Address: _____

EDUCATIONAL BACKGROUND

Highest Public School Grade Attended:_____Date: _____

Highest College or Vocational Grade Completed:_____Date:_____

Major in Public School:_____Minor:_____

Major in College or Vocational:_____Minor: _____

PERSONAL REFERENCES

NAME AND OCCUPATION	ADDRESS	PHONE
1.		
2.		
3.		

PRIOR WORK HISTORY (List in order, last or present employer first)

Name of Employer: _____

Address of Employer:_____

Dates Employed: From_____To_____

Reason for Leaving: _____

Name of Employer: _____

Address of Employer:_____

Dates Employed: From_____ To_____

Reason for Leaving: _____

Name of Employer: _____

Address of Employer: _____

Dates Employed: From_____ To_____

Reason for Leaving: _____

May we contact the employers listed above?_____. If not, indicate below which one(s) you do not wish to have contacted.

_____

Return to:

John Doe, Ph.D.
2810 Ethel Ave.
Suite 2
Muncie, Indiana 47304

SAMPLE 11

WAGE AND SALARY HISTORY FORM

EMPLOYEE NAME   PAYROLL NUMBER

	CONFIDENTIAL WAGE / SALARY HISTORY																
REASON FOR CHANGE																	
RATE OF PAY — PER																	
RATE OF PAY — AMOUNT																	
WORK LOCATION																	
POSITION AND CLASSIFICATION																	
DATES — TO																	
DATES — FROM																	

SAMPLE 12

WORK ATTENDANCE FORM

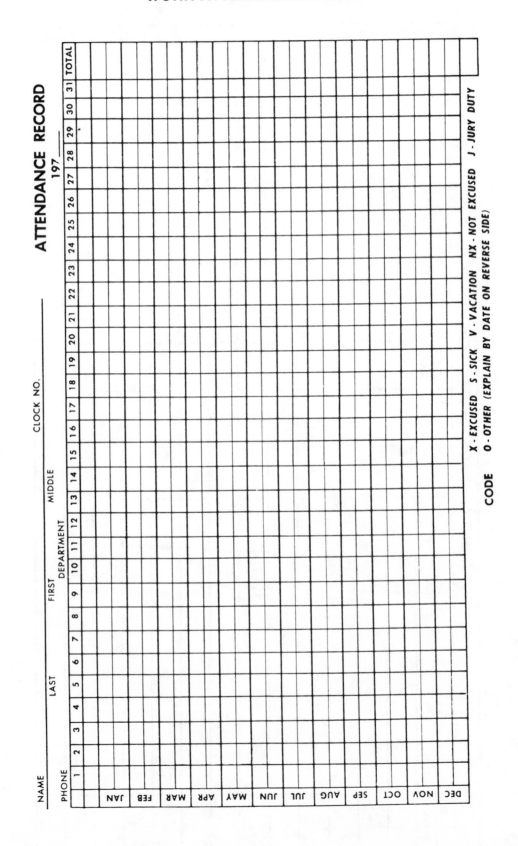

SAMPLE 13

CONSULTING CONTRACT

AGREEMENT OF PROFESSIONAL ASSOCIATION

This agreement is made this_____day of_____, 19___, by and between the John Doe, Ph.D. 2810 Ethel Ave., Suite 2, Corinthian Building, Muncie, Indiana 47304, Delaware County, Indiana, hereinafter referred to as the Clinic and_____of _____hereinafter referred to as the Consulting Therapist. This contract is to take effect immediately upon execution and is to continue in full force and effect through the_____day of_____, 19___, subject to prior termination as hereinafter provided.

The purpose of this agreement is to establish a contractual relationship between the Clinic and the Consulting Therapist whereby the Consulting Therapist may utilize certain business services and the physical facilities of the Clinic while the Consulting Therapist conducts his profession as an independent practitioner.

The clause headings appearing in the agreement have been inserted for the purpose of convenience and ready reference. They do not purport to, and shall not be deemed to, define, limit or extend the scope or intent of the clauses to which they appertain.

The parties to this agreement, in consideration of mutual covenants and stipulations set out herein, agree to the provisions of the following sections:

SECTION I

CONSTRUCTION. (1) Any masculine pronoun used herein refers to the Consulting Therapist, even if the Consulting Therapist is of the female sex. (2) A therapy hour consists of a minimum of fifty (50) minutes and a maximum of sixty (60) minutes.

SECTION II

NONASSIGNMENT. It is hereby agreed that the obligations assumed by each party herein are personal in nature, and that there will be no assignment or transfer of this contract, nor of any interest in this contract.

SECTION III

NO PARTNERSHIP. Nothing in this agreement is intended to, nor shall be deemed to, constitute a partnership or joint venture between the parties.

SECTION IV

NO AGENCY. It is agreed and understood that the Consulting Therapist is not the agent or employee of the Clinic; neither is the Clinic the agent or employee of the Consulting Therapist. The Consulting Therapist is engaged in his profession as an independent practitioner, and shall not represent otherwise to any third parties. There shall be no withholding for Consulting Therapists' tax purposes for monies collected by the Clinic and paid over to the Consulting Therapist. The Clinic promises and agrees to save harmless the Consulting Therapist from its acts or omissions resulting in liability. The Consulting Therapist promises and agrees to save harmless the Clinic from his acts or omissions resulting in liability.

SECTION V

NULLIFICATION OF PRELIMINARY NEGOTIATIONS. This contract constitutes the entire agreement between the parties hereto. It is agreed and distinctly understood that all previous communications and negotiations between the parties, either verbal or written, not contained herein, are hereby withdrawn and annulled.

SECTION VI

FACILITIES AND SERVICES PROVIDED BY THE CLINIC. The Clinic hereby undertakes to furnish to the Consulting Therapist office space in its physical plant located at 2810 Ethel Ave., Suite 2, Corinthian Building, Muncie, Indiana 47304, Delaware County, Indiana, on an appointment basis. It is understood that such office space is to consist of offices not assigned to personnel of the Clinic. It is further understood that determination of preference regarding office space among Consulting Therapists is to be made on a first come, first served basis.

It is further agreed that the Clinic shall provide certain business services to the Consulting Therapist. Such services shall include the processing of the billing operation, the maintenance of accounts receivable records, the maintenance of appointment schedules and the collection of patient charges.

SECTION VII

DUTIES AND RESPONSIBILITIES OF CONSULTING THERAPIST. It is the responsibility and obligation of the Consulting Therapist to make certain that each patient appointment is made with the secretary of the Clinic. Further, the Consulting Therapist must inform the secretary of the Clinic as to the type of therapy conducted with each patient.

The Consulting Therapist agrees to be, and is, responsible for the preparation and mailing of all follow-up letters directed to patient referral sources.

The Consulting Therapist agrees to notify the Clinic of any planned absences, including vacations, at least one (1) week in advance of such absence.

It is agreed that all forms provided the Consulting Therapist by the Clinic must be completed and submitted weekly to the Clinic. Such forms include, but are not limited to, Therapy Summary Sheets and Termination Sheets. Upon the failure of the Consulting Therapist to timely submit any forms so furnished, the Clinic is hereby empowered to withhold any monies due the Consulting Therapist but unpaid by the Clinic.

SECTION VIII

TERMINATION. This contract shall terminate and expire on the completion of the contract term herein provided. It is further agreed that this contract shall be terminated upon the Clinic's discontinuance or cessation of conducting a business which affords psychiatric services. This contract shall also terminate upon the cessation of the Consulting Therapist to engage in a profession related to psychiatry or psychology. Either the Clinic or the Consulting Therapist may terminate this contract by delivering written notice of intent to terminate to the other party thirty (30) days before such termination becomes effective.

SECTION IX

SAVINGS CLAUSE. Should any section or any part of any section hereof be declared to be invalid by a Court of competent jurisdiction, those sections and parts of sections of this contract not so declared to be invalid, shall remain in full force and effect for the duration of the contract.

SECTION X

RENEWAL. At the expiration of the term of this agreement of professional association, this agreement may be renewed by mutual consent of the parties hereto.

IN WITNESS WHEREOF, the parties have solemnly executed this agreement of professional association at Muncie, Indiana on the day and year first mentioned herein.

_____
AUTHORIZED AGENT OF CLINIC

_____
CONSULTING THERAPIST

SAMPLE 14

FEDERAL REGULATIONS

The authors wish to thank the directors of the Indiana State Chamber of Commerce for providing us with a general outline of material for this section of our book. The following items are federal laws. Check with the Attorney General's office of your particular state to obtain local ordinances which also apply.

POSTING AND RECORD-KEEPING REQUIREMENTS

FEDERAL

1. **Minimum Wage—Overtime—Equal Pay**: A poster entitled "Notice to Employees" is required of all employers under the Fair Labor Standards Act.

2. **Age Discrimination in Employment**: "The Age Discrimination in Employment Act Poster" is required of all employers, employment agencies, and labor organizations of 20 or more employees in industry or serving industry affecting interstate commerce.

3. **Government Contracts**: The poster "Notice to Employees Working on Government Contracts" (Walsh-Healey) must be posted in any establishment performing government contract work. It must also be posted by all contractors and sub-contractors who enter into any agreement with the federal government in excess of $2,500 for the principal purpose of furnishing services (Service Contract Act). "Handicapped. You have job rights!" (WH Pub. 1406) must be posted by federal contractors, in excess of $2,500 pursuant to Sec. 503 of Rehab. Act of 1973.

4. **Equal Employment**: Employers with 15 or more employees are required to display the poster "Equal Employment Opportunity Law."

SAMPLE 15

FEDERAL REGULATIONS

Statute	Records to be Retained	Period of Retention	Form of Retention
Fair Labor Standards Act (Wages and Hours)	a. For each employee: Basic payroll records, including name, home address, date of birth if under 19, sex and occupation, start of workweek (time and day), total wages paid each pay period, date of payment and period covered, basis of payment (e.g. "$450/month" or "$2.25 an hour").	a. **Three years:** Basic payroll records (see "Records to be Retained"), relevant union or individual employment contracts, applicable certificates and notices of Wage-Hour Administrator, sales and purchase records.	No particular form is specified. **Microfilm** is permissible if employer is willing to make any required transcripts. **Punched tape** is permissable if records can be readily converted to reviewable form.
	b. For each nonexempt employee: Regular hourly rate of pay for any week in which overtime occurs.	b. **Two years:** Basic time and earnings cards, wage rate tables, worktime schedules, shipping and billing records, records of additions to or deductions from wages.	

SAMPLE 15

FEDERAL REGULATIONS

Statute	Records to be Retained	Period of Retention	Form of Retention
Title VII of Civil Rights Act (Fair Employment Practices)	a. Any personnel or employment record made or kept by employer, including application forms and records having to do with hiring, promotion, demotion, transfer, layoff or termination, rates of pay or other terms of compensation, and selection for training or apprenticeship.	a. **Six months** from date of making the record or taking the personnel action involved, whichever occurs later.	No particular form is specified. Records as to racial or ethnic identity may be obtained either by visual survey or by maintenance of post-hire records where permitted by state law; such post-hire records should be kept separate from employee's basic personnel records available to those responsible for personnel decisions.
	b. Personnel records relevant to charge of discrimination or action brought by Attorney General against employer, including, for example, records relating to charging party and to all other employees holding similar positions, application forms or test papers conpleted by unsuccessful applicant and by all other candidates for same position.	b. Until final disposition of charge or action.	
	c. Those required to file apprenticeship reports shall maintain (1) chronological		

SAMPLE 15

FEDERAL REGULATIONS

Statute	Records to be Retained	Period of Retention	Form of Retention
Title VII of Civil Right Act (Fair Employment Practices)	list of names and addresses of all applicants, date of application, sex and minority group identification or (2) file a written applications containing same information.	c. Application forms or lists shall be retained for **two** years from date of application or, if annual report is required by Commission, two years or period of successful applicant's apprentice-ship, whichever is longer; other records made solely for purpose of completing reports to EEOC shall be retained for one year.	

SAMPLE 15

FEDERAL REGULATIONS

Statute	Records to be Retained	Period of Retention	Form of Retention
Age Discrimination Act	a. Payroll records containing each employee's name, address, date of birth, occupation, rate of pay, and compensation earned per week.	a. **Three years.**	a. and b. No particular forms specified.
	b. Personnel records relating to (1) job applications, resumes, or other replies to job advertisement including records pertaining to failure to hire; (2) promotion, demotion, transfer, selection for training, lay-off, recall, or discharge; (3) job orders submitted to employment agency or union; (4) test papers in connection with employer-administered aptitude or other employment test; (5) physical examination results; (6) job advertisements or notices to employees regarding openings, promotions, training programs, or opportunities for overtime work.	b. **One year** from date of personnel action to which record relates except 90 days for application forms and other preemployment records of applicants for temporary jobs.	
	c. Employee benefit plans, written seniority or merit rating systems.	c. Period plan or system is in effect plus one year.	

SAMPLE 15

FEDERAL REGULATIONS

Statute	Records to be Retained	Period of Retention	Form of Retention
Employee Retirement Income Security Act			

Employers are urged to check further on the recordkeeping requirements under this law with their employee benefits consultant and/or legal counsel. This is a relatively new enactment and more details may be forthcoming.

Sec. 107. Every person subject to a requirement to file any description or report or to certify any information therefor under this title or who would be subject to such a requirement but for an exemption or simplified reporting requirement under section 104 (a) (2) or (3) of this title shall maintain records on the matters of which disclosure is required which will provide in sufficient detail the necessary basic information and data from which the documents thus required may be verified, explained, or clarified, and checked for accuracy and completeness, and shall include vouchers, worksheets, receipts, and applicable resolutions, and shall keep such records available for examination for a period of not less than six years after the filing date of the documents based on the information which they contain, or six years after the date on which such documents would have been filed but for an exemption or simplified reporting requirement under section 104 (a) (2) or (3).

SAMPLE 15

FEDERAL REGULATIONS

Statute	Records to be Retained	Period of Retention	Form of Retention
Occupational Safety and Health (OSHA)	Form 100, Log of Occupational Injuries and Illnesses; Form 101, Supplementary Record of Occupational Injuries and Illnesses, and For 102, Summary, Occupational Injuries and Illnesses.	**Five Years.**	No particular form is specified.

SECTION VI

REFERRAL SYSTEM

NOTES

SECTION VI

REFERRAL SYSTEM

I. Establishing Referral Systems Prior to Opening Your Office

A. Whether one is familiar with the community or not, the **Telephone and Social Service Directory** are necessary tools to compile a comprehensive list of all the professional agencies that might make possible referrals.

B. The next step after a list is compiled is to categorize items on the list by means of labels such as governmental vs. non-governmental, large industrial firm vs. small business, private vs. public, and so forth.

C. Still another way of categorizing possible sources of referrals is under (the label) **rehabilitation,** which would include vocational rehabilitation, medical psychology, and crippled children's services. The next category might be **religious agencies,** such as Catholic Social Services, Lutheran Social Services, Jewish Social Services, Religious Counseling Agency, children's homes, or group homes maintained and established by the church. **Maintenance-type programs** might be the Welfare Department, Retardation Association, Sheltered Workshops and so forth. Private facilities might include group treatment homes, institutions, hospitals, private counseling centers or clinics, and any other agency that might be significant for a particular community, such as agencies dealing with drugs, alcohol, crisis, women's abuse centers, women's centers, and abortion clinics.

D. Once the agencies have been selected and placed in proper categories, it is then necessary to find out the director and/or administrator of each agency. Each individual's name, specific or general information about the individual and the agency, address, and phone numbers should be recorded and filed for future reference.

E. A **contact** should be made with a director or administrator if it is felt that his or her agency might make **direct referrals**; for example, vocational rehabilitation agencies could refer for testing or counseling treatment. The Welfare Department also might refer children or adults for psychological testing and possible treatment. Drug Center, Alcohol Center, and Women's Abuse Center might only be interested in some type of direct consultation in helping them to deal directly with their clientele in establishing a treatment program for them. Family Counseling Service might be interested only in testing, and a group home might be interested in either making direct referrals for individualized treatment or in establishing consultation and group treatment either with the staff or with the clientele. Mental Health Association will make direct referrals for psychotherapy and hospitalization.

F. Once this knowledge is obtained a visit should be made to the appropriate person's office.

G. During the visit, a **brochure** describing activities should be given to the administrator so that he or she can better understand your policy regarding the treatment procedure. Also, at that time, your **fee schedule** and opportunities for a working relationship might be discussed. In addition you might discuss follow-up procedure— being able to communicate with that agency about the individuals after they have been referred. In other words, **confidentially** and **releases of information** should be discussed so there is no misunderstanding in the future concerning your follow-up procedure.

H. If at all possible, when talking with the administrative director, you should request a **meeting with the staff** at one of the regular staff meetings so that you can explain your clinic or office to them (i.e. your particular qualifications, your general or specialized practice, and questions and answers). This would assure that all individuals within that agency have information about you and your office—because some administrators tend to hold back sharing that type of information because they know their employees would like to refer and, of course, this might cost their agency some funds since they might be in a position to reimburse for the fees concerning treatment or evaluation sessions.

I. Agencies such as YMCA or YWCA, Boys Clubs, Red Cross, Girl Scouts, Boy Scouts, and Cancer Society should be contacted concerning your establishment of a private practice, and a **brochure** should be sent to them with a **cover letter** stating that you would be willing to come to their office and talk individually with them or meet with their board of directors to discuss your particular operating procedure.

J. The social organizations within the community, such as Ministerial Associations, the Kawanis, Rotary, and other community organizations should be informed of your facility. You can make yourself available for **lectures** in regard to such topics as "what is psychotherapy," "new trends in the are of mental health," "biofeedback," "hypnosis," and other topics. Such groups generally will make use of an opportunity to have an expert come in and talk to them.

K. It should be noted here that this type of **free volunteer service** can be initiated easily at the beginning of the private practice; however, once the practice is established and the clientele and waiting list are established, such free time becomes harder and harder to find in your schedule.

L. Physicians should be contacted by sending out a **professional announcement**. Also, any type of letter or brochure that might explain in detail the procedure of your office or a policy statement and program description would be helpful in letting them know the type of services you plan to offer.

M. It is mandatory to make yourself available to such groups as the local medical society, hospital staff meetings, and the local family practice residency program when they have a meeting, as they will provide a large referral source for you.

N. Still another way of providing information concerning a facility is through being **interviewed** by the local newspaper or radio/TV station concerning some phase of mental health and psychotherapy or your opinions about abused wives, treatment of children, new methods of biofeedback, or the utilization of hypnosis in psychotherapy. However, this **should not** be solicited on your behalf. Only if you are called upon to be interviewed should you consider making yourself available for comment. If possible, you should ask to read the article before it is published so that you are not misquoted—which may do more damage than good.

O. Contact with the local police department, prosecutor's office, and/or sheriff's department is something that you might find beneficial inasmuch as they do have contact with individuals who are seeking assistance for problems. Also, you may want to develop workshops that could benefit the legal profession and society, such as, Driving While Intoxicated, Check Deception, Criminal Conversion, Public Intoxication and Disorderly Conduct Rehabilitation Program.

P. Generally, each of the local industries has representatives who either try to deal with personal-social problems or to make referrals. In some cases, this is a plant physician or nursing staff; in other cases it is the personnel director or the newly created "Employee Assistance Program or EAP" for salaried and hourly employees. A contact can be made with these individuals, and generally proper referrals can be secured. Also, do not hesitate to contact the union officials to talk with them, describing in detail your facility and type of services you will offer in the future.

Q. When possible, all surrounding community professionals (the physicians, ministers, mental health associations, and other social service organizations) should be sent **announcement cards.**

R. In smaller surrounding communities, most of the physicians will attend the hospital staff meetings, will welcome the opportunity of hearing from outside individuals about new facilities, and would like to know about them so that they have a place to refer their patients.

S. A form could be developed and sent to the potential referral source (mental health workers, physicians, ministers, etc) to aid them in the referral process. Along with the **referral form** a **cover letter** could be sent in order to explain how to utilize the form. Several copies of the form could be mailed or hand delivered to the referral source— as long as the referral source has asked or agreed to use the form. The form itself could include but not limited to the following: **(see page 74).**

II. **How to Maintain A Proper Referral System**

A. Once the practice and patient caseload is established and a potential waiting list is created, the need for working on a referral system is not as necessary. However, you should always be on guard to **protect** the **referral system** you have created.

B. A good way of being able to know your referral source is to keep some type of frequency count and data sheet concerning your referrals, i.e., who made the referral, why, when, etc. **Sample 63, page 159-160. Sample 51, pages 143-144.**

C. It is necessary to obtain a **release of information** form from each patient so that communications between you and the referring person can be established.

D. Once the release of information form has been signed, a letter stating that the individual was seen by you, the **follow-up letters** concerning progress, diagnosis, and prognosis, should be sent. However, sometimes only the initial letter has to be sent, since it is not always appropriate to send additional letters concerning the progress of the patient. Later on in this manual, this type of letter is described in detail.

E. Certain types of referral systems should be maintained over a long period of time, such as volunteering to train the individuals who work with Crisis Hotline or Drug Treatment Centers. This generally requires a small amount of time and effort on your part and may reap benefits in terms of the referrals that you will receive from them. Of course, the best and most significant referral agent you can establish is a **satisfied patient** who describes the treatment process and talks quite highly of your professional ability and makes direct referrals to you of friends, relatives, and the people he or she serves.

REFERRAL FORM INFORMATION

1. General Information
   (A) Name of referral source
   (B) Patient name, address, age and phone number
2. Problem Areas
   (A) Evaluations
   ____Educational Assessment
   ____Learning Disability Assessment
   ____Psychological and Behavioral Assessment
   ____Neurological Assessment
   ____Court Assessment
   ____Industrial-Personnel Assessment
   ____Disability Determination Assessment
   (B) Marriage and Family Problems
   ____Marital
   ____Family
   ____Parenting Skills
   ____Communicating Skills
   ____Separation/Divorce Coping
   (C) Problems of Children and Adolescents
   ____Developmental/Intellectual Assessment
   ____Problem Behavior: School and/or Home
   ____Behavior Therapy
   ____Enuresis/Encopresis
   ____Abuse
   (D) Sexual Problems
   ____Sexual Problems: Treatment for Individuals
   ____Sexual Problems: Treatment for Couples
   ____Incest/Abuse
   ____Others
   (E) Anxieties and Phobias
   ____Personal/Interpersonal Anxiety
   ____Lack of Assertiveness
   ____Stress Management
   ____Fears and Phobic Reactions
   (F) Depression
   ____Depression
   ____Inadequate Self-Regard
   ____Dealing with Loss
   (G) Substance Abuse
   ____Drug Dependency and Abuse
   ____Alcohol Abuse
   ____Tobacco Smoking
   ____Weight Control Program
   ____Eating Disorders
   (H) Other Problems
   ____Psychophysiologic Disorders
   ____Tension and Migraine Headaches
   ____Tics-Habits
   ____Self-Management
   ____Adjustment Problems
   ____Vocational Problems
   ____Miscellaneous Problems (Use AdditonalComments)
3. Additional Comments
   (A) Generally this is at least two lines in length for the purpose of writing comments.
   (B) This could be placed on the form or carbon copy so that the patient can not read the comments.
4. Feedback Desired
   (A) No feedback desired
   (B) Inform me as to whether my patient came to you for services.
   (C) Send me a report upon intake, an interim report, and a discharge report
   (D) Other, Please instruct. (This may or may not appear on the patient's copy.)
5. Referral Release
   (A) Optional
   (B) Should have signature of a witness.
6. Back side of referral form
   (A) Who is John Doe, Ph.D.?
   ____Basic data
   ____Personal vs. professional
   (B) What does John Doe, Ph.D. do?
   ____Educational testing and assessment
   ____Psychological assessment
   ____Individual, couple, marital, family, adolescent, child, and group therapy
   ____Hypnotherapy
   ____Biofeedback Training
   ____Relaxation Training
   ____Stress Management
   ____Weight Control Programs
   ____Smoking Control Programs
   ____Alcohol Abuse Programs
   ____Drug Dependence and Abuse Programs
   (C) How Are Appointments Made?
   ____Accepts self-referrals
   ____Referrals by professionals
   (D) How is the office financed?
   ____Self-pay by patients
   ____Supported by patient insurance coverage
   ____Privately owned
   (E) What Fee is charged for services?
   ____Fees are average for private mental health services
   ____Details may be obtained by calling for information
   ____Many health insurance plans have paid for the services of a psychologist
   ____Fees are deductible for income tax purposes
   (F) List of Staff
   (G) Map for Location

SECTION VII

ADMINISTRATIVE INTAKE

AND

OFFICE PROCEDURE

NOTES

SECTION VII

ADMINISTRATIVE INTAKE AND OFFICE PROCEDURE

I. Referral

A. All therapists must rely upon having other professionals or former patients refer patients to their private practices in order to maintain a proper caseload. In order to receive referrals, you have to maintain an open communication line and be willing to work with a wide variety of problems and pathology. This also means you must be available for emergency service in the evening and weekends. Once other professionals know that **you are reliable**, they will be willing to make direct referrals. Furthermore, once you have established yourself as being successful in working with difficult patients, professionals will continue to make referrals, as will your former patients.

B. Once a referral has been made and the patient has been in for the intake, a **letter** or **thank you card** should be sent to the referring professional saying that the patient kept the appointment. Of course, the patient should sign a release of information form before a letter is sent. This letter should be brief and inform the referring person of the following: (1) the patient kept the appointment; (2) what therapist the patient will see for therapy; (3) the date and time of next appointment; (4) a statement that a letter of progress will be sent in the future; and (5) thank the referring person for the referral. It should be noted that the referring individuals, especially the medical profession, wants feedback on their patient. The mental-health profession in the past has neglected this most important area of communication. **Samples 16-17, pages 79-80.**

C. After the patient has been properly diagnosed and a **treatment plan** has been established, then a second letter should be sent to the referring individual. This letter would inform the individual of the following: (1) any change of therapist and why; (2) progress being made or not being made; (3) diagnosis in descriptive terms; (4) a prognosis and possible length of treatment; and (5) any other significant information.

D. A letter should be sent after therapy has been **terminated**—termination by the patient, by the therapist, or by mutual agreement. This letter should state the following: (1) when the treatment was terminated; (2) who terminated; (3) progress made during the treatment; (4) condition of patient at the time of termination; (5) any follow-up that needs to be made by the physician or other professionals; (6) if the patient is open to return for treatment in the future; and (7) thank the referring person for making the referral.

II. Patient Appointment

A. A patient can be **self-referred** or **referred** by a professional. If the patient is referred by a professional, once the name and phone number are obtained, the patient is called to confirm the appointment. The patient is then instructed to come 30 minutes before the appointment so that an intake interview can be completed before the appointment begins.

B. The patient's **name** and **phone number** is put on the therapist's schedule. Either the letter "I" (for intake) or DI (for direct intake) should be placed next to the name on the schedule. **Sample 18, page 81.**

C. If possible, the patient is sent a **brochure** which describes the policy and procedure of the private practice. **Sample 26, pages 90-94.**

III. Administrative Intake

A. Once the patient arrives for the scheduled appointment and reports to the receptionist, the patient will complete the intake form.

B. There are two (2) color-coded **intake forms** —one for adults, one for children. Basic information is obtained, including name, address, place of employment, social security, insurance and ID information. **Samples 19 and 20, Pages 82-85.**

C. After the intake form has been completed, the receptionist or therapist determines (by employer insurance coverage) if the patient has **insurance** or is **self-pay**. (Of course, insurance companies will not reimburse for certain types of out-patient treatments.) Then the patient is given an out-patient payment schedule. **Samples 21-23** (color-coded), **pages 86-87.**

On one side of the **out-patient payment schedule** is an explanation of the insurance and information about what is covered for professional services; on the other side is a complete fee schedule of professional services. **Sample 24, page 88.** (For a sliding scale for professional fees, see **Sample 25, page 89.**

D. Next, the patient may be given a **psychological test,** such as an MMPI Booklet, MMPI Answer Sheet and/or Personal Data Sheet. The patient is given directions for completing the form and asked to complete it as soon as possible.

E. In closing the intake process, the receptionist or therapist **answers all questions** and gives the patient a brochure which explains the policy of the private practice: namely, the purpose, services available, intake procedure, length of treatment, missed appointment policy, answering service, paying your bill, sick leave, concluding remarks, list of staff, a map and appointment card. The patient is asked to read the policy statement so that there will be no misunderstanding. If the patient is from out of town, the policy statement is sent to the patient before the appointment, so that he or she can understand the procedure, have a map for directions to the office and an appointment card as a reminder of the day and time of the appointment. **Sample 26, page 90-94.**

F. The intake form is placed in a file folder and the secretary-receptionist then types a **bill** from the information on the intake form, including the name, address, phone number, date of birth, and insurance numbers. The secretary also types the patient's name and therapist's name on the file form or card. **Sample 27, page 95.**

G. The secretary **codes** the bill and file with a label. **Sample 28, page 96.**

H. The secretary also stamps the file **"Confidential Statement"** in red ink. **Sample 29, page 96.**

I. During this waiting period, the patient can listen to a **pre-training tape** for patients, which will describe for the patient what to expect of the therapy process. This type of pre-training helps the patient to understand what to expect and may answer questions the patient is afraid to ask. The patient can listen to the tape either in an available office or by earphone in the waiting room. If a tape is unavailable, the patient can read the office procedure and policy information during this time.

SAMPLE 16

**REFERRAL
THANK YOU LETTER**

PSYCHOLOGISTS ASSOCIATES
John Doe, Ph.D.
PSYCHOLOGIST
DIPLOMATE IN COUNSELING PSYCHOLOGY, ABPP

JANE DOE, M.A.
THERAPIST

March 3, 19____

John Doe, M.D.
Medical Arts Building
Suite 203
418 E. McGalliard
City, State   Zip

                              Re: Jane Doe
                                   R.R. 2, Box 30
                                   City, State   Zip

Dear Dr. Doe:

The above named patient was seen on this date at Psychologists Associates for her first appointment. The focus of the session was that of a psychological evaluation for the purpose of determining treatment procedure.

She gave a history of a recurrence of nervous reaction characterized by restlessness, worry, despondency and poor sleep. Mrs. Doe notes that her mother had a nervous condition of a rather similar type characterized by excessive worry; the mother was in her forties. I think, as well, it is noteworthy, that Mrs. Doe's mother died about a year and a half ago and subsequent to that her symptoms of general depressive feelings have increased in severity and caused her to seek treatment.

I plan to follow Mrs. Doe on a weekly basis with individual psychotherapy and she has a scheduled appointment with me next week on the 9th of March. I will continue to keep you informed of her progress and any change of treatment plan.

Thank you for referring this interesting patient.

                              Sincerely,

                              John Doe, Ph.D.
                              Psychologist
                              Diplomate in Counseling Psychology, ABPP

SAMPLE 17

REFERRAL
THANK YOU CARD

Thank You

FOR REFERRING _____

TO ME FOR PROFESSIONAL SERVICES.

YOUR EXPRESSION OF CONFIDENCE IS SINCERELY APPRECIATED.

_____

John Doe, Ph.D.
2810 Ethel Ave.
Suite 2
Corinthian Building
Muncie, Indiana 47304

Telephone 317-282-2863

SAMPLE 18

WEEKLY SCHEDULE

Week of: _____   Therapists: _____

Hour	Monday	Tuesday	Wednesday	Thursday	Friday	Saturday	Sunday
8 A.M.							
9 A.M.							
10 A.M.							
11 A.M.							
12 P.M.							
1 P.M.							
2 P.M.							
3 P.M.							
4 P.M.							
5 P.M.							
6 P.M.							
7 P.M.							
8 P.M.							
9 P.M.							

SAMPLE 19
INTAKE FORM FOR ADULTS
ADULT INTAKE SHEET   DATE:_____/_____/_____

Legal Name: _____
                      Last   First   Middle Initial

Address: _____
                      Number   Street   City   Zip

Phone: _____Age: ____Birthdate:_____/_____/_____Marital Status: _____

SS #:_____Employment:_____Date Last Worked:_____/_____/_____

Spouses Legal Name (and address if different): _____
                                                          First   Middle Initial

_____
           Number   Street   City   Zip   Phone

Age:_____Birthdate:_____/_____/_____Employment:_____

Responsible Party: _____Phone:_____

Address: _____
                      Number   Street   City   Zip

Close Friend: _____
or Relative   (optional)   Phone

Previous Professional Help:_____yes_____no   If yes, Name: _____

_____/_____/_____
                                                                          Date Last Seen

Psychiatric Hospitalization (Where & When): _____

_____

Personal Physician: _____
                                        Name   City

Referral Source:_____

Permission to contact all of the Above Mentioned Professionals:_____yes_____no

On Psychiatric Medication Now:_____yes_____no If so, name of medication: _____

_____

Medication Allergies: _____

Child's Name	Age	Living at home	Other Information

Blue Cross & Blue Shield: _____

Legal Name   Control No.

_____/_____/_____/_____/_____

I.D. No.   Benefit Code   Plan   SVC No.   Effective Date

Medicaid or Medicare: _____

Name of Insured

_____/_____/_____

I.D. No.   Med. Resources   Birthdate

Other Insurance: _____

_____

Intake Therapist: _____ First Appointment____/____/____

Information Gathered By:_____MMPI#_____S.C.:_____

Other Data: _____

_____

_____

SAMPLE 20
INTAKE FORM FOR CHILDREN

CHILD INTAKE SHEET

DATE:_____/_____/_____

Name: _____ Age:_____ Birthdate:_____/_____/_____
      Last   First   Middle Initial

Birthplace: _____ Phone:_____

Lives with: _____ Relation:_____

Address: _____
      Number   Street   City   Zip

Child is Natural: _____ Adopted:_____Other:_____

Natural Father: _____ Address:_____Phone:_____

Father's Employment: _____ SS #: _____ Birthdate:_____/_____/_____

Natural Mother: _____ Address: _____ Phone:_____

Mother's Employment: _____ SS #: _____ Birthdate:_____/_____/_____

Close Friend or Relative:_____
      Full Name   City   Phone

Step-Father: _____ Address:_____Phone:_____

Employment: _____ SS #:_____ Birthdate:_____/_____/_____

Step-Mother: _____ Address:_____Phone:_____

Employment:_____ SS #: _____ Birthdate:_____/_____/_____

Responsible Party: _____
      Name   Address   Phone

Employment: _____

Is Child currently attending school:_____yes_____no Present Grade level: _____

Where attending: _____ If not attending, Why:_____

_____

Previous Professional Help:_____yes_____no If yes, Physicians Name: _____

_____
      Address   City

Psychiatric or Psychological Hospitalization (Where & When): _____

Is the child on medication:_____yes_____no If yes, name of medication: _____

Medication Allergies: _____

Child's Physician: _____
Name   City

Referral Source:_____ Permission to contact all of the above professionals:
_____yes_____no

Siblings	Age	Living at Home	Other Information

Blue Cross & Blue Shield: _____
Name of Insured   Control No.

_____/_____/_____/_____/_____

I.D. No.	Benefit Code	Plan	SVC No.	Effective Date

Medicaid or Medicare: _____
Name of Insured

_____/_____/_____

I.D. No.	Med. Resources	Birthdate

Other Insurance: _____

_____

Intake Therapist: _____First Appointment:_____/_____/_____

Information Gathered By:_____MMPI #:_____S.C.:_____B.C.L.: _____

Other Data: _____

_____

_____

SAMPLE 21

LARGE NATIONAL AUTO CORPORATION
OUTPATIENT PAYMENT SCHEDULE

The coverage, which is for $1,000.00 per person per year for those covered under this program, begins January first and ends December thirty-first of each calendar year. If you should exceed the $1,000.00 limit but continue your therapy, you are responsible for any charges incurred. It is to your advantage to keep track of the charges and to be aware of when your Blue Cross coverage expires. If, after your Blue Cross has reached its maximum, you do not have a secondary coverage, you will be expected to pay at least one-half of the charge after each session, and a payment at the end of each month when you receive a bill in the mail.

SAMPLE 22

LARGE NATIONAL CORPORATION OUTPATIENT
PAYMENT SCHEDULE

The first $50.00 per person deductible must be paid by the patient before we can bill the insurance company. If you and your family are being seen, you must pay the first $125.00 before we are allowed to bill the company. After the initial deductible has been paid, the insurance company pays 50% thereafter and the patient pays the other 50%.

The deductible should be paid in full upon completing the second session. It is best that you obtain an insurance application that has been filled out and signed in the proper places and then turn it over to our insurance clerk as soon as possible. To avoid later confusion as to what you owe, and what your insurance owes, it is helpful if you pay your portion after each session. Be sure to have a signed, filled-out insurance form on file with us at all times.

SAMPLE 23

SELF-PAY OUTPATIENT
PAYMENT SCHEDULE

For people who have no insurance or who have insurance but are not sure as to its coverage, we suggest the following:

Make a payment after each session. It should be the full amount if possible, and if not then at least 50% of it. If you have insurance that may pay a large percentage of the bill, the clinic will reimburse you immediately upon receiving the check from your insurance company for whatever amount has been paid by you. If you have a balance due at the end of the month, when we send out statements you will be expected to make that payment as well as your regular payment after each session.

For those of you with insurance, please fill out the form where required, sign it in the proper places, and turn it in to our insurance clerk the first time in, and not later than the second session. Keep a completed form on file with us at all times.

For those of you without insurance coverage and who do not want to be billed at home, please keep your bill paid in full.

SAMPLE 24

FEE SCHEDULE APPEARS ON THE BACKSIDE
OF EACH OUTPATIENT PAYMENT SCHEDULE

Individual Therapy	$55.00
One half session	34.00
One qtr. session	19.00
Individual Therapy	
with Co-therapist	67.50
One half session	38.00
Marital Therapy	60.00
One half session	34.00
Marital Therapy	
with Co-therapist	85.00
Family Therapy	60.00
One half session	34.00
Family Therapy	
with Co-therapist	85.00
Group Therapy—per hr.	25.00
(min. 2 hrs.)	
Hypnotherapy	55.00
One half session	31.50
One qtr. session	17.50
Medication Check	25.00
Intake Testing	50.00
Psychiatric & Psychological	
Testing-Full Battery per hr.	50.00
(min. 4 hrs.)	
Telephone Therapy	25.00
Relaxation Tape	15.00

Each separate Outpatient Payment Schedule is color
coded to assist the Intake Process

SAMPLE 25

SLIDING SCALE
FOR
PROFESSIONAL SERVICES

*WEEKLY FEE SCHEDULE PER SESSION

FAMILY INCOME

NUMBER OF DEPENDENTS

Weekly Pay	Monthly Pay	Yearly Pay	1	2	3	4	5	6	7 and over
$ 58-115	$ 250-499	$ 3,000- 6,000	15.00	14.00	13.00	12.00	11.00	10.00	10.00
116-173	500-749	6,000- 9,000	20.00	19.00	18.00	17.00	16.00	15.00	15.00
174-288	750-1,249	9,000-15,000	25.00	24.00	23.00	22.00	21.00	20.00	20.00
289-384	1,250-1,666	15,000-20,000	30.00	29.00	28.00	27.00	26.00	25.00	25.00
385-576	1,667-2,500	20,000-30,000	35.00	34.00	33.00	32.00	31.00	30.00	30.00
577-769	2,501-3,333	30,000-40,000	40.00	39.00	38.00	37.00	36.00	35.00	35.00
770 and above	3,334-and above	40,000-and above	50.00	49.00	48.00	47.00	46.00	40.00	40.00

*Some use this fee schedule for individual therapy with additional charge for marital/ family therapy—while others do not charge for additional individuals per session.

SAMPLE 26

POLICY STATEMENT OF PROFESSIONAL SERVICES

PSYCHOLOGISTS ASSOCIATES

2810 Ethel Avenue • Suite 2 • Corinthian Building • Muncie, Indiana 47304 • 317/282-2863

The following policy statement can easily be modified to meet individual needs as it relates to a psychiatric, clinical psychology, counseling psychology and/or social work private practice.

NEW PATIENTS

Your decision to enter into psychotherapy was undoubtedly a serious one arrived at after considerable thought. Whether you wre referred to us by your physician, urged to seek counseling by family or friends, or came because of problems and feelings only you know about, the decision to come here was yours.

Purpose of Psychologists Associates

The function of Psychologists Associates and its staff is to help you resolve problem areas in your life. Although no one can solve your problems for you, we are usually quite successful in helping people cope with their own difficulties. Your therapist will be an understanding person who is interested in helping you work through your emotional distress. It is the function of the therapist to listen, to understand, and to be helpful to the fullest extent of his or her professional training. It is your responsibility to help the therapist understand your life situation, thoughts, and feelings, and to have the courage to try to master problem areas. Your relationship with your therapist is confidential. No information concerning you will be released without your consent. If you were referred to us by a physician, however, we will obtain your medical records and inform him or her of your general progress from time to time, although not necessarily revealing details which you might prefer remain confidential. You will be asked to sign a release of information form at the time of your intake for the obtaining and releasing of your medical history and the general progress of your therapy. You have a right to refuse to sign the release of information form if you so desire.

Services Available

Psychologists Associates provides a variety of services. Individual, marital, family, and group therapy are offered along with hypnotherapy and biofeedback training. Medication and hospitalization can be arranged if needed. In addition, Psychologists Associates conducts, when necessary, psychological and educational testing and evaulation. These services are available to everyone—children, adolescents, and adults. There are no eligibility requirements for therapy. People may refer themselves for help, or they may be referred by a physician, a minister, a school principal, an attorney, an employer, friends, or family.

Intake Procedure

Once you decide to seek help, telephone 282-2863 for an appointment. On the day of your first appointment, you will spend a short time with the receptionist or therapist who will explain the charges and your particular insurance program and its coverage for therapy. Next you will see a therapist who will discuss with you your problem and how the staff might be able to assist you.

Length of Therapy

Therapy does not provide instant answers, but sometimes situational problems can be dealt with in relatively short periods of time. The frequency of your visits should be determined by you and your therapist sometime during the first three therapy sessions. Usually after six or eight sessions, you and your therapist will discuss your progress and prognosis. You have the right, at any time, to discontinue treatment whether or not your therapist agrees with your decision. Termination, however, should always be discussed with your therapist in a straightforward manner before you decide to discontinue therapy.

Missed Appointments

Psychological clinics differ in many respects from other medical and paramedical clinics. Unlike non-psychiatric physicians, osteopaths, dentists, and other professionals who operate on more flexible and inexact schedules, we psychotherapists commit a specific time period (usually 50 minutes) to each patient. It is therefore important that you appreciate the fact that a block of time has been set aside for you. Our schedules are usually crowded. Your cancelling or rescheduling appointments without sufficient notice usually means the loss of an hour of therapy, as it is difficult to reassign the hour to someone else on short notice. To be sure, we all occasionally "forget" appointments or are incapacitated and are unable to attend them. But whenever possible, we would appreciate 48 hours notice if you cannot attend the hour of therapy for which you have contracted. Rescheduling will be done for you in cases of emergency. At the end of each therapy hour, we will try to schedule your next appointment at a time convenient for you.

Missing Two Sessions

If you should miss two appointments without notice, whether because of your negligence, your aversion to dealing with certain feelings, or inconsideration of the importance of the therapeutic hour, you will be billed $25.00 for the second hour missed. This fee must be paid before you will be scheduled for future therapy. Billing for missed appointments is not covered by insurance—and must be paid by you personally. Your refusal to comply with this request will result in the termination of your therapy. Should this happen, you may request your therapist to refer you to some other source of therapy in your area.

Answering Service

Psychologists Associates has an answering service available at all time. During regular working hours, a receptionist will answer the telephone, but after normal working hours, the answering service will take calls. If you telephone after normal working hours but no one answers, **call back in a few minutes**. The answering service will take your message and relay it to a therapist. Please reserve after-hours calls for emergencies and save non-emergency problems for your next therapy session. Occasionally, a patient takes advantage of the answering service by turning a call into an over-the-phone therapy session. If that should happen, a charge will be added to his or her bill.

Paying Your Bill

Please try not to let your bill become burdensome; we suggest that you budget regular payments toward it so that it does not become a financial problem. Should you have trouble meeting he costs of therapy, please discuss your situation with your therapist or the receptionist. Therapy rates and insurance programs which cover outpatient treatment will be discussed with you by the therapist or receptionist at the time of your first session.

Sick Leave

Sick leaves from work are sometimes suggested by the staff, providing that they are warranted by clinical evaluation. They will not, however, be made retroactive to cover prolonged periods of absence from work before evaluation. Sick leaves are not given as a matter of course, and they should never be taken for granted as a part of therapy. Should you be placed on sick leave, you will be expected to attend **all therapy sessions** scheduled, as sick leave requires continued supervision. Your failure to do so shall result in the immediate termination of your sick leave. If you are currently under a physician's care and are on sick leave, please inform your therapist. Also inform him or her if you have been missing work but are not under a physician's care. Should you be placed on sick leave, the therapist will assume responsibility for your absence from work only for specific periods of time. Should you fail to return to work upon the expiration of your sick leave, the therapists will not assume responsibility for your absence.

Concluding Remarks

Therapy is a two-way effort entailing mutual respect, responsibility, and consideration between you and your therapist. The policies outlined above are designed to make your therapy productive and to avoid any unnecessary problems. Should you have questions about any policy, whether mentioned here or not, please feel free to discuss them with your therapist or the receptionist. By working together, we can establish a rewarding therapeutic relationship.

PSYCHOLOGISTS
ASSOCIATES
2810 ETHEL AVE.
SUITE 2
CORINTHIAN BUILDING
MUNCIE, INDIANA 47304
317/282-2863

* * *

PROFESSIONAL STAFF

John Doe, Ph.D.   Jane Doe, Ph.D.
Psychologist   Psychologist

* * *

CONSULTING STAFF

Jane Doe, MA
Therapist

PSYCHOLOGISTS ASSOCIATES
2810 ETHEL AVE.
SUITE 2
CORINTHIAN BUILDING
TELEPHONE 282-2863
MUNCIE, INDIANA 47304

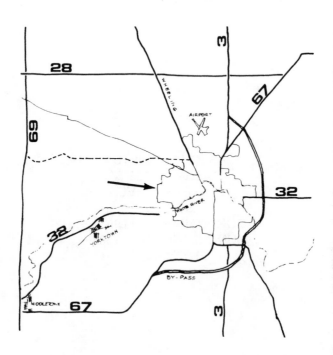

M _____

HAS AN APPOINTMENT ON

☐ MON.   ☐ TUES.   ☐ WED.   ☐ THURS.   ☐ FRI.   ☐ SAT.

A.M.

DATE _____ AT _____ P.M.

PSYCHOLOGISTS ASSOCIATES
2810 ETHEL AVE.
SUITE 2
CORINTHIAN BUILDING
TELEPHONE 282-2863   MUNCIE, INDIANA 47304

IF 24 HOUR NOTICE OF CANCELLATION IS NOT RECEIVED
YOU WILL BE CHARGED FOR MISSED APPOINTMENT.

SAMPLE 27

PATIENT BILL

STATEMENT

John Doe, Ph.D.
2810 Ethel Ave.
Suite 2
Corinthian Building
Muncie, Indiana 47304

Phone 317/282-2863

Private Practice Certificate State Board of Examiners in Psychology Lic. No. 09-00083-1-72

DATE	FAMILY MEMBER	PROFESSIONAL SERVICE	CHARGE	CREDITS		BALANCE
				PAYM'TS	ADJ	
		BALANCE FORWARD				

1625

PAY LAST AMOUNT IN THIS COLUMN

BIO - BIOFEEDBACK
CON - CONSULTATION
CO - CO-THERAPIST
EC - ERROR CORRECTION
FT - FAMILY THERAPY
GT - GROUP THERAPY
HC - HOSPITAL CARE

HYP - HYPNOTHERAPY
IT - INDIVIDUAL THERAPY
IF - INSURANCE FORMS
ITT - INTAKE TESTING
MT - MARITAL THERAPY
MC - MEDICATION CHECK
MA - MISSED APPOINTMENT

NC - NO CHARGE
PCE - PSYCHIATRIC EVALUATION
PLE - PSYCHOLOGICAL EVALUATION
ROA - RECEIVED ON ACCOUNT
RT - RELAXATION THERAPY
TT - TELEPHONE THERAPY
TFB - TESTING-FULL BATTERY

SAMPLE 28

LABELS FOR CODING THE
PATIENT'S BILLS AND FILE

SELF PAY

BLUE CROSS

MEDICAID

MEDICARE

SAMPLE 29

FILE IS STAMPED WITH
CONFIDENTIAL STATEMENT

CONFIDENTIAL

This report must not be made
available to the patient or any
nonprofessional persons.

SECTION VIII

THERAPY INTAKE

AND

STAFFING PROCEDURE

NOTES

SECTION VIII

THERAPY INTAKE AND STAFFING PROCEDURE

I. Therapy Intake

A. The secretary informs the therapist that the patient's **administrative intake** has been completed.

B. The therapist gives a self-introduction and takes the patient(s) to a private office for the **therapy intake.**

C. The therapist interviews the patient to get a brief history of the presenting problem.

D. The therapist either will write intake notes on the second page of **Intake Form** or on the first page of the **Therapy Summary Form**—a diagnostic and prognostic impression should be made at this point for the purpose of billing the insurance company (if billing is possible). The diagnosis generally must correspond with the *Diagnostic Statistical Manual—Edition III (DSM III)* which is published by the American Psychiatric Association. **Sample 30, page 101** (the first page of the Therapy Summary Form) and **pages 102-103** (different examples of the second page of the summary sheet). Some individuals prefer a line on the form to limit the notes for each session.

E. After the session, the therapist fills out the **Service Rendered Form B** and gives it to the patient, who gives it to the receptionist—the therapist circles the services rendered (so the secretary knows what to charge) and indicates when he or she wants to see the patient again. This form also informs the therapist how much the patient owes, based on previous and current balances. **Sample 32, page 104.**

F. The patient goes back to the receptionist and turns in the **Service Rendered Form.** The receptionist at this time will collect on self-pay patients or have them sign insurance forms. The receptionist gives the patient the other side of the **Service Rendered Form A** so that the patient has a record of the current balance. **Sample 31, page 104.**

G. The receptionist also will give the patient an **Appointment Card** (as well as a business card) for the next appointment, indicating the day and time. The card also has the name of the therapist, address, phone number, and a statement concerning cancellation. **Sample 33, page 105** (example of an Appointment Card). **Sample 34 page 105** (example of an Business Card).

H. Each time the patient comes in for an appointment, the receptionist will **stamp the date** of patient contact on the **Treatment Summary Form.**

II. Staffing

If the patient is seen in a clinic setting, then a **staffing may be held** in order to discuss the patient's history; present exam and testing; diagnosis; prognosis and future treatment plan. The following outline might be utilized for staffing.

A. At the staffing the therapist provides a **case history** of the patient so that a proper assignment can be made, with consideration to such matters as diagnosis, treatment plan and any specialized treatment plan.

B. The receptionist then calls the patient and makes an appointment with the same intake therapist or a new assigned therapist.

C. The appointment is scheduled as soon as possible and recorded on the **therapist schedule. Sample 18, page 81.**

D. The remainder of the staffing is devoted to **problem cases** and **in-service educational training**—one or two hours per week is devoted to the staffing.

SAMPLE 30

PATIENT-CONTACT FORM

THERAPY SUMMARY FORM

THERAPISTS: _____

PATIENT'S NAME: _____ DATE: _____

DIAGNOSIS: _____ DATE: _____

PROGNOSIS: _____ DATE: _____

RECOMMENDATION FOR TREATMENT:

THERAPY UTILIZED

_____Indivdual Therapy

_____Group Therapy

_____Family Therapy

_____Marital Therapy

_____Multiple Therapy

_____Hypnotherapy

_____Hypnotherapy Tape

_____Relaxation Tape

_____Psychological Evaluation

_____Psychiatric Evaluation

_____Medication

_____Hospitalization

****TERMINATION****

DATE OF TERMINATION: _____ TOTAL NUMBER OF SESSIONS: _____

REASON FOR TERMINATION AND DISPOSITION: (circle one)

    1—Patient withdrew from service
    2—Terminated—no referral/open to return
    3—Terminated with referral
    4—Mutual termination

WAS PATIENT REFERRED TO ANOTHER THERAPIST OR AGENCY___YES ___NO

IF YES, WHO: _____

ADDITIONAL COMMENTS: _____

STATUS AT TERMINATION:

    1—Resisted treatment
    2—Lower level of functioning
    3—Unimproved in most areas
    4—Improved in most areas

    5—Generally higher level of functioning
    6—Fully functioning
    7—Psychiatric treatment not indicated
    8—Other _____

RE-OPENED DATE: _____

RE-TERMINATION DATE: _____ STATUS AT TERMINATION: _____

RE-OPENED DATE: _____

RE-TERMINATION DATE: _____ STATUS AT TERMINATION: _____

RE-OPENED DATE: _____

RE-TERMINATION DATE: _____ STATUS AT TERMINATION: _____

Date	Therapists	Session #	Comments	Page #_____
Date	Therapists	Session #	Comments	_____
Date	Therapists	Session #	Comments	_____
Date	Therapists	Session #	Comments	_____
Date	Therapists	Session #	Comments	_____

Date	Therapists	Session #	Comments

SAMPLE 31

SERVICE RENDERED FORM—A

RECEIPT NUMBER	DATE	DESCRIPTION—CODE	CHARGE	PAYMENT	CURRENT BALANCE

YOU PAID THIS AMOUNT_____

JOHN DOE, PH.D.
2810 ETHEL AVE.
SUITE 2
CORINTHIAN BUILDING
MUNCIE, INDIANA 47304

TELEPHONE 317-282-2863

Hours By Appointment

Consultation	Hospital Therapy	Medication Evaluation	Psychological Evaluation
Error Correction	Hospital Visit	Miscellaneous	Reports
Educational Evaluation	Insurance Forms	Marital Therapy	Received on Acct.
Family Therapy	Individual Therapy	Multiple Therapy	Relaxation Therapy
Group Therapy	Missed Appointment	No Charge	Telephone Prescription
Hypnotherapy	Medication Check-up	Psychiatric Evaluation	Telephone Therapy

This time is reserved for you. If 24 hour notice of cancellation is not received, you will be charged for missed appointment.

NEXT APPOINTMENT_____ AT_____
DATE   TIME

#11076

SAMPLE 32

SERVICE RENDERED FORM—B

PREVIOUS BALANCE	NAME

Please present this slip to receptionist before leaving office.

SERVICES RENDERED

CONS.	H.T.	M.E.	PS.E.
E.C.	H.V.	MISC.	REP.
E.E.	INS. F.	M.T.	R.O.A.
F.T.	I.T.	MUL. T.	R.T.
G.T.	M.A.	N.C.	TEL. PR.
HYPTN.	M.C.	P.E.	T.T.

TOTAL $

NEXT APPOINTMENT _____ AT _____
DATE   TIME

#11076

SAMPLE 33

APPOINTMENT CARD

M _____

HAS AN APPOINTMENT ON

☐ MON.   ☐ TUES.   ☐ WED.   ☐ THURS.   ☐ FRI.   ☐ SAT.

A.M.

DATE _____ AT _____ P.M.

PSYCHOLOGISTS ASSOCIATES

2810 ETHEL AVE.

SUITE 2

CORINTHIAN BUILDING

TELEPHONE 282-2863   MUNCIE, INDIANA 47304

IF 24 HOUR NOTICE OF CANCELLATION IS NOT RECEIVED
YOU WILL BE CHARGED FOR MISSED APPOINTMENT.

SAMPLE 34

BUSINESS CARD

TELEPHONE 317-282-2863

JOHN DOE, ED.D.

PSYCHOLOGIST
DIPLOMATE IN COUNSELING
PSYCHOLOGY, ABPP

PSYCHOLOGISTS ASSOCIATES

2810 ETHEL AVE.

SUITE 2

OFFICE HOURS
BY APPOINTMENT

CORINTHIAN BUILDING
MUNCIE, INDIANA 47304

NOTES

SECTION IX

THERAPY FORMS,

OFFICE FORMS,

AND

TERMINATION PROCEDURE

NOTES

SECTION IX

THERAPY FORMS, OFFICE FORMS AND TERMINATION PROCEDURE

I. Therapy Process-Cancellation

A. Once the patient is being seen on a regular basis, the **Therapy Summary Form** is completed by the therapist. **Sample 30, pages 101-103.**

B. If the patient calls in and cancels a session, this is marked on the **Therapy Summary Form** and **Weekly Schedule** as a **PC** (patient cancelled) and a **Cancellation Form** is completed by the receptionist and given to the therapist. **Sample 35, page 111.** This is also helpful if you are called into court to testify about dates or if a malpractice suit is filed against you.

C. If a patient fails to keep an appointment, it is recorded in the same way as above, except that it is listed as an **NS** (no show).

D. If the patient is covered by **insurance** or is **self-pay**, then a failure to keep the appointment notification is sent stating that the patient will be charged for missed appointments. **Sample 36, page 112.**

E. If the patient is covered by **Medicaid**, then a failure to keep your appointment notification is sent stating that the therapist will refer the patient to another therapist if he or she continues to miss future appointments. **Sample 37, page 112.**

F. One other type of cancellation occurs when the therapist has to reschedule a patient. This is referred to as **TRS** (therapist rescheduled). Or if the patient ask to be rescheduled, it is referred to as **PRS** (patient rescheduled).

II. Hospital Visits

A. If the therapist has **hospital privileges**, (either full privileges or consultation privileges), he or she can make case notes which can be transferred to the file. **Sample 38, page 113** (example of in-patient hospital record sheet).

B. Hospital visits should also be recorded in the **Therapy Summary Form**, and on the therapist's schedule. **Sample 30, pages 101-103, Sample 18, page 81.**

III. Release of Information

A. Patients at different times will request that you **transfer your records**, write a letter or send a social history to another professional. Whenever this occurs, you should protect yourself by having the patient sign an **Authorization To Release Information Form**. This protects you from future law suits concerning confidentiality. However, the letter or report should also be stamped as being confidential. **Samples 39 and 40, pages 114-115.**

B. Some patients will refuse to sign a **Release Of Information Form**. The patient's decision should be respected.

IV. Requesting Information

A. Generally, the therapist wants to request information from the referring person or from the family medical doctor or past therapist. In this case, have the patient sign the **Authorization To Transfer Medical Information. Sample 41, page 116.**

V. Requesting a Psychological Evaluation

A. If a patient wants **psychological testing** for himself or herself or for a child, it is proper to ask the patient to fill out a **Request Form**.The same is true (even more so) if the court or another agency is requesting you to do a psychological evaluation. **Sample 42, page 117.**

B. If a psychological evaluation is to be completed, then a **Social History Form** might be desirable. A great deal of family, environmental, and social information can be obtained if this form is properly utilized by the professional. **Sample 43, pages 118-124.**

C. A standardized format should be employed whenever writing up a **Psychological Evaluation. Sample 44, pages 125-129.**

VI. Termination

A. Whenever a patient is terminated by the therapist, referred to another agency, or decides not to return, a **Termination Form** should be completed and the file placed in the inactive file when the bill has been paid in full. **A Termination Form** is part of the **Therapy Summary Form. Sample 30, page 101.**

B. If a patient should return for therapy, then a **second termination** would be completed when the patient is terminated from treatment.

SAMPLE 35

CANCELLATION FORM

Date___/___/___

CANCELLATION

Therapist: _____

Patient: _____

Appt. Date: _____Time:_____

Rescheduled: Date: _____Time:_____

Will Call: _____No App't:_____

Message: _____

_____

_____

_____

Therapist Notified:

Date:_____Time:_____

Initials:_____

SAMPLE 36

FAILURE TO KEEP YOUR APPOINTMENT NOTIFICATION FOR INSURANCE AND SELF-PAY PATIENTS

Dear_____

    You failed to keep your appointment with your therapist. This card is to remind you that this missed appointment is a loss of both time and money. You will be charged in the future if you fail to keep your appointment. Your insurance does not cover this charge. If you cannot keep your next appointment, please call and notify us in advance.

SAMPLE 37

FAILURE TO KEEP YOUR APPOINTMENT NOTIFICATION FOR MEDICAID PATIENTS

Dear_____

    You failed to keep your appointment with your therapist. This card is to remind you that this missed appointment is a loss of both time and money. This may result in having your case referred to another therapist. Your Medicaid does not cover missed appointments. If you cannot keep your appointment, please call and notify us in advance.

SAMPLE 38

**IN-PATIENT HOSPITAL
RECORD SHEET**

HOSPITAL RECORD SHEET

Date:____/____/____Room No.:_____

Patient: _____

Referring M.D.:_____

Charge:_____For the Following: _____

_____

Diagnosis: _____

_____

Prognosis: _____

_____

Referred: _____

_____

_____

Therapy Notes: _____

_____

_____

_____

_____

_____

_____

_____

SAMPLE 39

RELEASING INFORMATION TO
ANOTHER PROFESSIONAL

AUTHORIZATION FOR RELEASE OF INFORMATION

I understand that in order to gain the most benefit from a treatment program it is essential that information be exchanged between person(s) involved in treatment and John Doe, Ph.D.

I, _____ , hereby

authorize _____ and other authorized Program personnel, in accordance with Federal Regulation, Part 1401, Title 21, of the Code of Federal Regulations (37CFR1401), and in compliance with Section 408 of Public Law 92-255 (21USC1175), to release the below specified, information from my records to

records to _____
(Name of person & organization)

_____, _____
(Address)   (Telephone No.)

This release shall be in effect for one year unless renewed or revoked in writing by patient.

Authorized information to be released: **YES   NO**

(a) Notification of initial contact   ___   ___

(b) General treatment information   ___   ___

(c) Periodic progress & evaluation reports   ___   ___

(d) Urinalysis &/or attendance reports   ___   ___

(e) General medical information   ___   ___

_____   _____ _____
Witness   Client Signature   Birth Date

_____   _____
Date Witnessed   Date Signed

SAMPLE 40

RELEASING INFORMATION TO
ANOTHER PROFESSIONAL

AUTHORIZATION FOR RELEASE OF INFORMATION

I, _____, being of

sound mind and fully cognizant of the consequences of my acts, do

hereby authorize and direct John Doe, Ph.D. to release and furnish any or

all information to _____regarding myself

and/or my condition(s) including, but not limited to, professional

opinions, reports of examination, tests, treatment, diagnosis and

prognosis.

Further, I hereby relieve John Doe, Ph.D. of any duty of confi-

dentiality in accordance with the provisions set forth herein. The fore-

going authority shall continue in force and effect until revoked by me in

writing.

Dated this_____day of _____, 19_____.

_____

PATIENT

_____

WITNESS TO PATIENT'S SIGNATURE

SAMPLE 41

REQUESTING INFORMATION FROM
ANOTHER PROFESSIONAL

DATE_____

AUTHORIZATION TO TRANSFER MEDICAL INFORMATION

TO WHOM IT MAY CONCERN:

I hereby authorize any physician, surgeon, hospital, psychologist, social worker, counselor and nurse, to furnish to John Doe, Ph.D., 2810 Ethel Ave., Suite 2, Corinthian Building, Muncie, Indiana 47304 any and all records, information and evidence in their possession regarding_____

_____

injuries, medical history, and physical condition both prior and subsequent to the above date, regardless of lapsed time.

Upon presentation of this authorization, or an exact copy thereof, you are directed to permit the personal review, copying or photostating of such records, information and evidence by any representative of John Doe, Ph.D.

_____
Witness

_____
SIGN

_____
DATE

SAMPLE 42

REQUEST FOR PSYCHOLOGICAL EVALUATION

I would like to request psychological testing for the following person:

Name:_____

Address: _____

Phone:_____Age:_____Date of Birth: _____

The parents are: Name: _____

               Address: _____

                       _____

               Phone: _____

The parents have agreed that their child should undergo psychological testing: Yes_____ No_____

The reason for psychological testing is:_____

_____

The following person will bring the youth in for testing:

_____Phone:_____

The referring individual is: _____

                            Phone:_____

The Social History and any other significant information must be received by the John Doe, Ph.D. before testing. Has the Social History and other material been sent? Yes_____ No_____

_____   _____
Date of Request   Signature of parent and/or
                               Administrative director of
                               Referring Agency

SAMPLE 43

SOCIAL HISTORY FORM

SOCIAL HISTORY

Identifying Data

Name: _____ School: _____

Address: _____ Grade: _____

Telephone No.: _____ Religion: _____

Race: _____ Referred by: _____

Date of Birth: _____

Age: _____

Current Family	Name	Relationship to Client	Age	Occupation or Grade
Father:				
Mother:				
Children:				

Natural Parents:

Married: _____ Separated: _____ Divorced: _____

Date _____ Date _____ Date _____

Others in Household	Relationship	Age

Early Development:

Birth—Was labor short, long or normal? Was it difficult or normal? Complications, if any? _____

Was the pregnancy planned? _____

What was the weight of the child at birth? _____ Length? _____

Approximate month of walking? _____ Talking? _____

Bowel Control? _____ Bladder Control? _____

What techniques, if any, were utilized in toilet training? _____

As a baby, was he/she a good eater? _____ Poor eater? _____

Any food allergies? _____ Strong dislikes? _____

Sleeping Pattern? _____

Play Pattern? _____

Was there anything unusual or significant that you can recall about this period of his/her life? _____

_____

Childhood:

How old when first separated from parents? _____

Length of time involved in separation experiences? _____

Who usually cares/cared for the child? _____

In terms of emotion, how did he/she express himself/herself when angry?

_____

When frustrated or under stress, does he/she fight, become immobile and/or run away from the situation? _____

Any childhood illnesses or injuries? _____

_____

School Experience and Adjustment

What does he/she like best about school? _____

What is most troublesome in school: teachers, studies, or other children?

_____

Has he/she ever changed schools or would he/she like to? _____

What kinds of things would be different at another school? _____

_____

Were there any occurrences of grade failure? _____

If so, do you recall the reason? _____

_____

Have you ever noticed any unusual ability in your child? _____

_____

Were there ever any indications of adjustment problems in school: for example, school phobia, truancy, or poor behavior? _____

_____

Did the schools, at any time, see the need to have your child tested? _____

If so, do you have any recollections of the type of test and the results?_____

_____

Peer Relationships:

Does he/she have one friend, a few best friends, or does he/she claim to have good social relationships with nearly everyone? _____

What is your understanding of the nature and depth of the relationships?_____

_____

Do they tell each other secrets? _____

_____

How often do they see each other? _____

What kinds of things does he/she do with his/her friends?_____

_____

Who are some of the other children that he/she does not like? _____

_____

What kinds of differences do they have? _____

_____

Does he/she belong to any clubs or groups? _____

_____

What seems to be his/her dominant range of activity and interest? _____

_____

What do you feel are his/her strongest assets and finest traits? _____

Health:

Have there been any particular illnesses or significant injuries in his/her life? _____

_____

Also, were there any complications as to the injuries or illnesses and what were their approximate durations?_____

_____

Has he/she ever been on any type of medication?_____

If so, define what it was, the amount and frequency/day_____

_____

To your knowledge, does he/she smoke, consume alcohol and has he/she experimented with drugs? (define frequency, type of drugs used, etc., in these categories)_____

_____

Relationship to siblings and parents:

How does he/she relate to his/her brothers/sisters (rivalries, jealousies)?_____

_____

If he/she had a problem, who would he/she feel most comfortable sharing it with—mom or dad?_____

Whom does he/she feel understands him/her the most—mom or dad? _____

If they wanted something to happen, whom do you think they would count on the most to get it accomplished—mom or dad? _____

What experiences, if any, has he/she had in earning money and/or holding a part-time job?
_____

What was done with the money which he/she earned? _____
_____
_____
_____

What is your understanding, as parents, of the problem which has led to your son/daughter being brought to the attention of juvenile authorities? (Ex. Meaning and significance of the behavior to the child, parents, and other family members) _____
_____
_____
_____

When do you think you first began to notice that something was wrong or when did his/her behavior change? (Ex. origin, severity and duration of difficulties) _____
_____
_____
_____
_____

How do the problems that you have been having with him/her compare to those of your other children? _____
_____
_____
_____
_____
_____
_____
_____

Parents' Marital History:

How old were you at the time of your marriage and what was the length of the courtship?
_____

What were some of the attitudes and reactions on both sides of the family to your marriage? _____

Who has assumed the dominant role in each of these areas:

Management of money_____

Discipline of children_____

Major decisions in family_____

What do you think attracted each of you to one another?

Husband _____

Wife _____

Have there been any other previous marriages for either of you?_____

If so, can you recall any particular reasons why the marriage/marriages ended in failure?

_____

_____

_____

Have you for any reason been separated during this marriage and, if so, what was the reason(s)? _____

_____

_____

If you have been separated, what was the length of separation(s) and with whom did the children stay? _____

_____

How did this child, in particular, as well as the others, react to this?

_____

_____

_____

Every family tries to establish its own rules and regulations. How are discipline and obedience taught in this home? _____

_____

_____

_____

_____

_____

Father's Personal History:

It is helpful to know your date of birth as well as the city and state in which you were born.

_____

If you have any brothers or sisters, what was your order of birth in the family?_____

Can you recall what your parents did for a living and do you have any recollection as to how they managed their financial problems? _____

_____

_____

_____

How have your brothers/sisters adjusted to adult life? (Ex. marriage, if any; occupation etc.?) _____

_____

In looking back at your own childhood and teenage years, were there any significant events, illnesses, or problems that you or any other family members encountered? _____

_____

_____

_____

_____

How best would you describe that period of time in your life, and why do you choose to describe it that way? (Ex. happy time, sad, difficult period, etc.) _____

_____

_____

_____

_____

How old were you when you left home? _____

How long have you worked at your current job, and what is your present salary level? _____

What, if any, previous jobs have you held? _____

_____

_____

_____

Mother's Personal History:

It is helpful to know your date of birth and the city and state in which you were born.

_____

If you have brothers and sisters, what was your order of birth in the family? _____

_____

_____

Can you recall what your parents did for a living, and do you recall how they handled their financial problems? _____

_____

_____

How have your brothers/sisters adjusted to adult life? (Ex. marriage, if any; occupations, etc)? _____

_____

_____

In looking back on your own childhood and teenage years, were there any significant events, illnesses, or problems that you or any other family member encountered? _____

_____

_____

How best would you describe that period of time in your life and why do you choose to describe it that way (Ex. happy time, sad, difficult period, etc.) _____

_____

_____

How old were you when you left home? _____

How long have you worked at your current job, and what is your present salary income?

_____

What, if any, previous jobs have you held? _____

_____

Describe your house and the type of neighborhood that you live in. (Ex. number of rooms, who shares bedrooms, etc., do the children walk or take a bus to school) _____
_____
_____

What are your own parents' interests and activities (social clubs, sports, hobbies)? _____
_____
_____

How frequently, if at all, have you moved as a family?_____
_____
_____

SAMPLE 44

EXAMPLE OF A
PSYCHOLOGICAL EVALUATION

NAME: John Smith
ADDRESS: 407 N. White St.
   Old Castle, Indiana
MOTHER'S NAME: Mrs. Mary Smith
MOTHER'S ADDRESS: Same
DATE OF BIRTH: 2/18/63
SEX: Male
RACE: Caucasian

SCHOOL LAST ATTENDED:
   Old Castle Community School
GRADE LAST ATTENDED: 8th
CHARGE: Incorrigible
DATE OF TESTING: 8/19/77
FILE CODE NUMBER: 1653
REFERRING AGENCY: John Doe, M.D.

REASON FOR REFERRAL:

John Doe, M.D. referred John Smith for a psychological and educational evaluation relative to the disposition of his case by County Juvenile Court.

BACKGROUND INFORMATION:

John Smith is a 14 years and 6 months old boy, born in Old Castle, Indiana, who currently lives with his mother, Mary Smith, in Old Castle. John's mother is approximately 40 years old, is unemployed, and has completed ninth grade and is receiving ADC. John has two brothers and one sister, one half-brother and one half-sister. One sister (21) is not at home; one sister (17) is at home, but is not enrolled in school; one brother (16) is currently in detention. The other four children range in age from 5 to 12 and in grades from Kindergarten to 7th. John's father, Jim Smith, left his family fourteen years ago and currently lives in another state. John's father and mother are not divorced. Besides the above members of the household, John's mother has a male friend who has been living with the family for about seven years. John has been attending Community middle School in Old Castle and is currently awaiting transfer to another eighth grade class within that school.

John's prenatal and developmental histories appear to be unremarkable. He weighed approximately 8 pounds when born. He walked at one year and talked at two years. John's mother stated that he has had no significant illnesses or injuries. She stated that he likes sports, particularly baseball. His grades in school have been below average. She stated that his main problem in school has been poor behavior and some truancy. She said that John has a few good friends who he sees every day, but she did not know what they did together. She stated that John has "always seemed to have problems." When discussing his present trouble, she said that John was put in detention for 45 days because of disorderly conduct, public intoxication, theft, and some other charges which included assault and battery. She also said he has had many previous charges.

John appears to have been in trouble since February, 1972 (when he was 9), with cases of theft, assault and battery, possession of stolen property, incorrigibility, house burglary, and other charges up to the present charge. It appears that in each charge John was placed under advisement, or warned and released. In October, 1973 (when he was ten), the school corporation filed a petition which charged John with "being incorrigible, ungovernable and beyond the control of school officials." John has a long history of aggressive behavior and fighting in school. Recommendations were made by the probation officer in 1973 and 1974 that John be placed in a private institution. The second time, according to the Probation Office report, "John was released from the detention center to go with his mother, pending placement at a private institution. The family left the state and did not return until last year." On his return, John was re-admitted to middle school, but eventually was excluded from some classes and the cafeteria due to disruptive behavior. After being involved in theft and assault and battery, he again was recommended for placement in a private institution, which at the time had no openings from that time to the present.

PSYCHOMETRIC DATA:

(a) Past testing:

Information from the Probation Office stated that in 1973 John's I.Q. was reported to be 70 and that he was working below his grade level. Information as to when the test was given and what type of test instruments were used was not available.

(B) Present testing:
1. Intelligence testing:

(a) Weschsler Intelligence Scale for Children-Revised

Norms: National

	Scaled Score	I.Q.
Verbal	23	67
Performance	8*	44*
Full Scale	*	*

*Not considered to be representative of John's abilities (See Interpretation and Evaluation).

2. Peabody Picture Vocabulary Test

3. Wide Range Achievement Test

4. Hooper Visual Organization Test

5. Development Test of Visual-Motor Integration

6. Bender Visual-Motor Gestalt Test

7. House-Tree-Person Test

8. Rotter Incomplete Sentences Test

9. Dvorine Pseudo-Isochromatic Plates (See Interpretation and Evaluation)

10. Visual Screening (See Interpretation and Evaluation)

11. Hearing Screening (See Interpretation and Evaluation)

12. Tapping Board Test (possible indication of brain pathology)

13. Hand Dynamometer Test (within normal limits)

14. Social History

15. Diagnostic Interview

INTERPRETATION AND EVALUATION:

Results of the intellectual testing done indicate that John's present verbal functioning I.Q. is approximately 67, which, according to Wechsler's classification of intelligence, falls within the range "mental defective." John showed an ability to work arithmetic problems in his head at a low average level. He was deficient in his ability to demonstrate general knowledge, define words, and understand similarities and social situations. There were indications of cultural/educational deprivation. John's ability to manipulate objects, to understand part-whole relationships, and demonstrate awareness of cause/effect sequences appeared to be severely impaired. This possibly could be due to poor visual perception, double vision or moderate brain damage. He appeared to be trying hard during the test session, but did not seem aware of what was wrong with the pattern he was working with, such as a puzzle or design. In these types of tasks, he did not match up small pieces in any logical order or arrangement.

John demonstrated a significant deficit in academic functioning related to his age and grade placement. He was able to achieve a reading recognition grade equivalent level of approximately middle fourth grade, spelling at beginning third grade level, and arithmetic at a middle third grade equivalent level. He made an attempt to sound out words and spell phonetically. His handwriting was legible, but he wrote "M" when it should have been "N" (traim for train) and spelled "shaut" for "shout". In reading, he would change the internal vowel, reading "grave" for "grieve," "spill" for "spell". In arithmetic, he was unable to add large columns of numbers or perform any operations with fractions. However, his standard scores on the achievement tests ranged from 66 to 74, which correlates with his Verbal I.Q. score of 67. It is suggested that John actually performed on the achievement tests at a level in accordance to his potential.

Perceptual motor tests indicated severe perceptual motor difficulties, possible moderate organic brain pathology and/or visual difficulty, including possible blurred or double vision. John had difficulty organizing parts to make a whole, difficulty in copying geometric figures in a structured setting (he was only able to work on this task in a manner expected of an average 6½ year old child), difficulty in making simple drawings, and difficulty in maintaining proper size orientation. John took a long time to complete his copying and his drawings and he appeared to be concentrating intensely on the task at hand.

Projective and personality tests indicated that John was feeling large amounts of tension, anxiety, and frustration. There were indications of aggressiveness, acting-out potentials, difficulties with handling aggression, and fears of emotional expression. He exhibited feelings of depression and low energy levels. He exhibited difficulty with concentration, confusion and disorientation. He demonstrated dependent feelings and a need for warmth and support. He demonstrated a tendency to withdraw or to handle frustration with aggression.

John appeared to be concentrating on tasks at hand and spent a long time, when allowed, to complete tasks. He wanted to do some tasks by himself, rather than be helped by having the exercises read to him. He often became absorbed in what appeared to be irrelevant details and appeared to lose track of what he was supposed to be doing. He had difficulty remembering the year in which he was born and the place where he lived. He did not make any spontaneous comments during the testing session. He made frequent erasures, but when given a new eraser, he kept forgetting to use it and returned to the old one. He constantly was rubbing his head and tilting his head back, but denied having trouble with vision or a headache. He appeared to be highly distractible. If someone walked by outside the building, he looked up and lost track of what he was doing.

SUMMARY:

John is a 14 years, 6 months old boy who has been in trouble with authority figures since he was nine. His present verbal functioning I.Q. is approximately 67. John appears to have severe perceptual motor difficulties and visual and perceptual distortions, so much so that it was considered impossible to get a valid performance I.Q. score. He was able to achieve grade equivalent levels at third to fourth grade in reading recognition, spelling and arithmetic computation. He indicated feelings of tension, anxiety, and frustration. He was highly distractible and had difficulty keeping his attention focused on the assigned task.

In spite of all his difficulties with visual distortion, perceptual motor difficulties, and distractibility, John appeared to concentrate hard on the presented tasks and was able to achieve at a level commensurate with his intellectual potential. It is suggested that he has been incapable of doing academic tasks at the level of his class placement and that this, along with perceptual distortions and lack of warmth and emotional support and low self-assurance, could be causing feelings of extreme frustration which are being released in aggressive and anti-social behaviors.

The hearing and Dvorine did not indicate any impairment; however, John failed to pass the visual examination and it is suggested that he be referred for further testing.

RECOMMENDATIONS:

1. It is strongly recommended that John be placed in an environment where he can receive warmth and emotional support accompanied by firmness and a necessity to face the consequences of his behavior. This would need to be a highly structured, totally restrictive environment, initially where John would have to earn privileges by acceptable behavior. At the same time, a total structure and placement in an environment where he can possibly achieve (e.g., third grade materials, nondistracting setting), might help reduce his anxiety and frustration levels to where they can be more easily handled both by John and his teachers/counselors. At John's present level of intellectual functioning and level of frustration, it is suggested that he does not have the ability to learn from his mistakes merely by being told not to do it again or by being removed from the situation in which he is being disruptive.

2. It is recommended that John be referred for a complete neurological examination by a neurologist.

3. It is recommended that John be referred for a complete visual examination by an opthamologist.

4. It is recommended that John not be returned to his home environment, but be placed in a restrictive environment pending his placement, even if this takes a long time.

5. It is recommended that the probation officer remain concerned about John's placement until it is accomplished.

6. If it is impossible to keep John in detention, or find placement for him in a highly structured environment, it is recommended that he be put on restrictions as much as possible and be forced to earn "privileges with good behavior." For example, he could be required to check in with the probation officer every day after school or required to bring notes of attendance and good behavior from the school. It also would be important to talk with John's teachers to make sure the level of work presented to him is at his ability level (approximately third grade).

7. It is recommended that the final disposition of this case be contingent upon John's behavior in the future, i.e., after he has been in a restrictive structured environment for at least two years.

_____   _____
Date Submitted   Name of Psychologist and
                                           License Number

NOTES

SECTION X

INTERNAL ACCOUNTING

AND

OFFICE PROCEDURE

NOTES

SECTION X

INTERNAL ACCOUNTING AND OFFICE PROCEDURE

I. Billing of Self-Pay Patients

A. During the **intake procedure**, the receptionist and/or therapist will need to discuss the fee schedule. If the patient's insurance policy does not cover out-patient treatment, then the fee schedule along with a payment schedule is discussed in detail. Any questions that the patient wants to ask are answered by the receptionist and/or therapist. **Sample 23-24, pages 87-88.**

B. After the patient begins therapy, **a bill is established for future billing**. The patient is requested to make at least partial payment after each visit and a minimum of one payment per month. Since the patient comes to therapy with problems, it seems inappropriate to add another problem, a financial one. Your patient should be able to pay the bill without causing his or her family unnecessary financial difficulties. However, the best practice is to have the patient pay the bill in full after each session if insurance does not cover full or partial payment.

C. The **first billing** of a self-pay patient is sent out **within** the **first thirty** (30) **days** after therapy is initiated. The billing procedure includes making a copy of the actual bill and mailing it to the patient—some patients request that the bill not be sent to their home or that the envelope not have the name of the therapist on the outside. The therapist should adhere to the request of the patient concerning the envelope not having the name on the outside. Nevertheless, the bill will be sent to the patient if a payment is not made after a proper length of time. However, an efficient method of handling that is to establish a post office box and printing only this box number as a return. The receptionist and/or therapist will do everything possible to assist the patient by discussing the bill with the patient when he or she comes in for therapy, or by making a personal telephone call to the patient, or by reducing monthly payment so that the patient can meet his or her obligation. If the patient meets the monthly payment after the bill is sent out, then this same procedure is followed on a monthly basis. **Sample 45, page 136 and Sample 46, page 137.**

D. If no payment is received within thirty (30) days after the first billing, then a **letter is sent** to the patient within **the next thirty** (30) **days.** This letter is not meant to intimidate the patient; moreover it asks the patient to disregard the letter if he or she has simply overlooked paying the bill, misplaced the bill, or already paid it. **Sample 47, page 138.**

E. If the patient refuses to pay by ignoring the first billing and the first letter, then a second letter is sent. This letter is sent as the **FINAL NOTICE** and asks the patient to check an appropriate financial agreement, sign it, and send it back to the office. **Sample 48, page 139.**

F. If the patient refuses to sign the **FINAL NOTICE,** or signs it, but does not make a payment, then the final procedure is implemented: a copy of the bill is sent again, and **PAST DUE** IS STAMPED ON THE BILL (in **red ink**) **Sample 49, page 140.**

G. After the bill with the red ink message is sent, a **personal phone call** is made to the patient so that he or she is completely aware of the consequences of not making a payment.

H. If no payment is received within a two week period, then the patient's bill is turned over to the **collection agency**. This is especially true of patients who have terminated therapy and make no effort to be responsible in meeting their obligation.

I. If the patient is **unable to pay** in any circumstances, then there is the possibility of **writing the bill off as a bad debt.** However, your accountant should assist you in determining when and when not to turn an individual over to a collection agency and when to write off an unpaid bill as a loss.

J. Generally, it is better to **put an upper limit on how high the patient's bill can rise** before taking action in terms of sending the letters, making a personal phone call, or turning the account over to the collection agency.

II. Billing the Patient's Insurance

A. If a patient is **fortunate** enough **to have excellent out-patient coverage**, then the insurance company generally prefers that the therapists fill out the insurance reimbursement form and receive the payments directly.

B. The receptionist, of course, will need all of the insurance **identification information** (benefit code number, ID number, and effective date), as well as the number of sessions to be billed (obtained from the patient's bill).

C. There is generally an **upper limit on each policy**; therefore, once that has reached its upper limit, the patient can request, if applicable, that the therapist bill his major medical insurance.

D. There should be **consistency in the billing of insurance companies**, particularly in the time of month the bill is sent out, in the checking of the patient's bill against the therapy notes and date of contact, and in whether or not proper charges were made in regard to the type of therapy administered. **Sample 55, page 183** (a reimbursement form from a major insurance company) and **samples 56 and 57, pages 184-185** (a reimbursement form for governmental health insurance).

III. Patient Billing His or Her Own Insurance

A. Some insurance companies and governmental insurance policies prefer that the **patient pay the bill** and personally send the form in for reimbursement.

B. If this is the case, then the **patient can fill out the form** or the receptionist can fill it out; however, some therapist charge a small fee for filling out the reimbursement form.

C. There is generally an **upper limit to a policy**; however, with some policies the patient can then transfer to his or her major medical policy.

IV. Internal Control

A. In order to maintain proper billing, the therapist should have several ways to **double-check the billing**. They are as follows:
1. The **schedule** will tell if the patient was in for the appointment;
2. The **therapy notes** along with the date of the session will verify the appointment;
3. The **bill** is still another way of recording the therapy, contact, date of contact, and the charge for professional services;
4. The **control** or **day sheet** which lists each patient seen for a given day is a way of verifying if a certain patient was seen and what the bill was.

B. In a large group practice or a practice owned by one therapist internal control must be utilized in order to safeguard the financial security of the practice. The receptionist, in order to **maintain internal control** of patient contact as it relates to the therapist's professional contract, keeps a **weekly statistical report** on each consulting therapist. The statistical report provides a complete breakdown of the number of patients who were seen, patients who cancelled, and the number of therapist cancellations. A form on actual income generated by each consulting therapist is the second page of this report. **Sample 50, pages 141-142.**

C. Another form is the **monthly statistical intake report.** This form also can be utilized for the end-of-the-year report of the number of intakes completed during a twelve month period. This monthly report not only provides all personal data (age, sex, and marital status), but also provides information about where the patient came from, how he or she was referred, and what the payment source for the patient was. This type of report can be compared on a monthly or yearly basis. This type of informaiton can assist in understanding possible trends, such as the number of intakes referred by a specific person or agency. **Sample 51, pages 143-144.**

D. In order to have each file completed (therapy notes, termination form completed, bill paid), the receptionist must review each form to make sure that everything is procedurally correct before it is filed in the inactive file. If there is inaccurate or insufficient information, then the **check sheet for effective communication form** is completed by the receptionist and attached to the file. The therapist then receives the file and corrects the necessary items and turns the file back to the receptionist. The receptionist double-checks the file and then places it in the inactive file. **Sample 52, pages 145-146.**

SAMPLE 45

PATIENT BILL WITH CHARGE-PAYMENT ENTRY

STATEMENT

PHONE NUMBER

DATE OF BIRTH

John Doe, Ph.D.
2810 Ethel Ave.
Suite 2
Corinthian Building
Muncie, Indiana 47304

Phone 317/282-2863

Hours by Appointment

- LAST NAME, FIRST NAME MIDDLE INITIAL
  STREET ADDRESS
  CITY, STATE ZIP CODE

- INSURANCE NUMBERS

NUMBER	DATE	DESCRIPTION	CHARGE	PAYMENT	CURRENT BALANCE
19____	1/7	I.T. 1 hr.	47 50		47 50
	1/14	I.T. 1 hr.	47 50		95 00
Ins Bill	1/15				
	1/21	I.T. 1 hr.	47 50		142 50
	1/28	I.T. 1 hr.	47 50		190 00
	1/30	R.O.A. - Insurance		45 00	145 00
	2/4	I.T. 1 hr.	47 50		192 50
Ins Bill	2/5				
	2/11	I.T. 1 hr.	47 50		240 00
	2/20	R.O.A. - Insurance		142 50	97 50
Ins Bill	2/21				
	3/3	R.O.A. - Insurance		47 50	50 00
Pt Bill	3/4				
	3/10	R.O.A. - Check Pt.		50 00	------

NOTE: IF A DAY SHEET SYSTEM IS BEING USED, THIS BILL WOULD BE HAND WRITTEN RATHER THAN TYPED.

PLEASE PAY LAST AMOUNT THIS COLUMN ☛

Consultation	Hospital Therapy	Medication Evaluation	Psychological Evaluation
Error Correction	Hospital Visit	Miscellaneous	Reports
Educational Evaluation	Insurance Forms	Marital Therapy	Received on Acct.
Family Therapy	Individual Therapy	Multiple Therapy	Relaxation Therapy
Group Therapy	Missed Appointment	No Charge	Telephone Prescription
Hypnotherapy	Medication Check-up	Psychiatric Evaluation	Telephone Therapy

**This time is reserved for you. If 24 hour notice ot cancellation is not received,
you will be charged for missed appointment.**

THIS IS A COPY OF YOUR ACCOUNT AS IT APPEARS ON YOUR LEDGER CARD

SAMPLE 46

PERSONALIZED BILL FOR AN INDIVIDUAL IN PRIVATE PRACTICE

STATEMENT

JOHN DOE, Ph.D.
2810 ETHEL AVE.
SUITE 2
CORINTHIAN BUILDING
MUNCIE, INDIANA 47304
317-282-2863

DATE _____

_____

_____

_____

FOR PROFESSIONAL SERVICES: $ _____

SAMPLE 47

LETTER INFORMING PATIENT OF LATE PAYMENT

PSYCHOLOGISTS ASSOCIATES
John Doe, Ph.D.
PSYCHOLOGIST
DIPLOMATE IN COUNSELING PSYCHOLOGIST, ABPP
Jane Doe, M.A.
THERAPIST

PATIENT'S NAME
ADDRESS

Balance Due $ _____

   In checking my files, I found that your bill has not been paid. If you have overlooked, mis-placed, or already paid, please disregard this letter. If you have received the billing and have not yet sent your payment, please do so in the very near future.

Sincerely,

John Doe, Ph.D.
Psychologist

SAMPLE 48

FINAL NOTICE TO PATIENT

PSYCHOLOGISTS ASSOCIATES
John Doe, Ph.D.
PSYCHOLOGIST
DIPLOMATE IN COUNSELING PSYCHOLOGIST, ABPP
JANE DOE, M.A.
THERAPIST

FINAL NOTICE

Patient's Name
Address

Amount Enclosed $_____

Balance Due $_____

Because your account is long past due, I would normally turn it over to a collection agency. I would, however, prefer dealing directly with you. Please read and check one of the three options below and return to us.

☐ 1. I would prefer to settle this account. Please find full payment enclosed.

☐ 2. I would prefer to make weekly/monthly payments of $_____until this balance is cleared up. I understand that no interest will be charged for this delayed payment schedule, and that the minimum weekly payment is $5.00 and the minimum monthly payment is $20.00.

☐ 3. I would prefer that you assign this account to an agency for collection. (Failure to return this past due reminder will result in this action.)

Signed: _____

If you have any questions, please do not hesitate to call me.

Sincerely,

John Doe, Ph.D.
Psychologist

2810 ETHEL AVENUE • SUITE 2 • CORINTHIAN BUILDING • MUNCIE, INDIANA 47304 • 317/282-2863

SAMPLE 49

PATIENT BILL WITH RED-INK DUE MESSAGE

STATEMENT

PHONE NUMBER

DATE OF BIRTH

John Doe, Ph.D.
2810 ETHEL AVE.
SUITE 2
CORINTHIAN BUILDING
MUNCIE, INDIANA 47304

TELEPHONE 317/282-2863

Hours by Appointment

- LAST NAME, FIRST NAME MIDDLE INITIAL
  STREET ADDRESS
  CITY, STATE ZIP CODE

- PATIENT HAS NO INSURANCE

031

NUMBER	DATE	DESCRIPTION	CHARGE	PAYMENT	CURRENT BALANCE
19_____	1/7	I.T. 1 hr.	47 50		47 50
	1/14	I.T. 1 hr.	47 50		95 00
	1/21	I.T. 1 hr.	47 50		142 50
	1/28	I.T. 1 hr.	47 50		190 00
Pt. Bill	1/30				
	2/4	I.T. 1 hr.	47 50		237 50
	2/11	I.T. 1 hr.	47 50		285 00
	2/18	I.T. 1 hr.	47 50		332 50
Pt. Bill	2/30				
Pt. Bill	3/30	1st letter			
Pt. Bill	4/30	2nd letter			
		An Audit Of Your Account Shows It Is PAST DUE. If this Account Is Not Paid Within 15 Days It Will Be Turned In For COLLECTION.			
NOTE:		IF A DAY SHEET SYSTEM IS BEING USED, THIS BILL WOULD BE HAND WRITTEN RATHER THAN TYPED.			

PLEASE PAY LAST AMOUNT THIS COLUMN ◄

Consultation	Hospital Therapy	Medication Evaluation	Psychological Evaluation
Error Correction	Hospital Visit	Miscellaneous	Reports
Educational Evaluation	Insurance Forms	Marital Therapy	Received on Acct
Family Therapy	Individual Therapy	Multiple Therapy	Relaxation Therapy
Group Therapy	Missed Appointment	No Charge	Telephone Prescription
Hypnotherapy	Medication Check-up	Psychiatric Evaluation	Telephone Therapy

**This time is reserved for you. If 24 hour notice of cancellation is not received,
you will be charged for missed appointment.**

THIS IS A COPY OF YOUR ACCOUNT AS IT APPEARS ON YOUR LEDGER CARD

SAMPLE 50

STATISTICAL REPORT ON PATIENT CONTACT BY EACH THERAPIST

FROM 6/1/_____

Minimum Required to Schedule	_____	BREAKDOWN FOR THE WEEK:	
Actually Scheduled	_____	Intakes	_____ hrs.
Hours Short or Long for the Year	_____	Multiples	_____ hrs.
Total Therapy Hours	_____	Regular Therapy	_____ hrs.
Total Bonus Hours	_____	Total Therapy Hrs.	_____ hrs.
Total Weeks Worked _____			

Average of Total Patients Hours   Seen_____   Scheduled_____

_____

FOR WEEK OF_____/_____/_____TO_____/_____/_____

	TOTAL WEEK	TOTAL YEAR	WEEK AVE.
Total Hrs. Scheduled	_____	_____	_____
Hrs. Short or Long from 26	_____	_____	_____
Over 20 Bonus Hours	_____	_____	_____
Total Pt. Contact Hrs.	_____	_____	_____
Total Pts. Seen	_____	_____	_____
Half-Hours	_____	_____	_____
Quarter Hours	_____	_____	_____
Intakes Scheduled	_____	_____	_____
Multiples Scheduled	_____	_____	_____
Special Rate Patients	_____	_____	_____
No Charge	_____	_____	_____
No Show	_____	_____	_____
Patient Cancelled	_____	_____	_____
Patient Rescheduled	_____	_____	_____
Therapist Cancelled	_____	_____	_____
Vacation Hours Used (running total)	_____	_____	_____
Sick Days Used (running total)	_____	_____	_____
Special Training Days Used (running total)	_____	_____	_____

FOR WEEK OF_____/_____/_____TO_____/_____/_____ (COMPLETED_____/_____/_____)

Regular Hours Scheduled	_____
Intakes Scheduled	_____
Open Hours Available	_____

FOR WEEK OF_____/_____/_____TO_____/_____/_____ (COMPLETED_____/_____/_____)

Regular Hours Scheduled	_____
Intakes Scheduled	_____
Open Hours Available	_____

Name of Therapist

Income that should be generated this week: _____hrs. x $55.00 =

_____

Actual income generated _____

Income generated since January 1st should total _____

Actual income generated since January 1st is_____
(Ahead) (Behind) _____for the year.

Name of Therapist

Income that should be generated this week: _____hrs. x $55.00 =

_____

Actual income generated _____

Income generated since January 1st should total _____

Actual income generated since January 1st is_____
(Ahead) (Behind) _____for the year.

Name of Therapist

Income that should be generated this week: _____hrs. x $55.00 =

_____

Actual income generated _____

Income generated since January 1st should total _____

Actual income generated since January 1st is_____
(Ahead) (Behind) _____for the year.

Name of Therapist

Income that should be generated this week:_____hrs.____ × $55.00 =

_____

Actual income generated _____

Income generated since January 1st should total _____

Actual income generated since January 1st is_____
(Ahead) (Behind) _____for the year.

SAMPLE 51

STATISTICAL MONTHLY INTAKE REPORT

MONTH _____19_____

Total Intakes for Month of_____19_____was _____

	TOTAL
SEX:	
Male _____	_____
Female _____	_____

IS A FAMILY MEMBER CURRENTLY OR PREVIOUSLY BEING SEEN:

Yes _____ _____

No _____ _____

Patient previous seen here _____ _____

MARITAL STATUS OF PATIENT:

Single _____ _____

Married _____ _____

Separated _____ _____

Divorced _____ _____

WHERE IS PATIENT FROM:

City _____ _____

County _____ _____

Madison County _____ _____

Henry County _____ _____

Jay County _____ _____

Randolph County _____ _____

Wayne County _____ _____

Grant County _____ _____

Blackford County _____ _____

Marion County _____ _____

Other _____ _____

REASON FOR REFERRAL:

Therapy _____ _____

Biofeedback _____ _____

Hypnosis _____ _____

Testing Only _____ _____

Consultation Only _____ _____

Court Evaluation Only _____ _____

Personnel Evaluation Only _____ _____

AGE RANGE OF PATIENT:

1- 5 _____ _____

6-10 _____ _____

11-15 _____ _____

16-20 _____ _____

21-30 _____ _____

31-40 _____ _____

41-50 _____ _____

51-65 _____ _____

Over 65 _____ _____

DIRECT REFERRAL TO:
    Dr. Smith _____ _____
    Dr. Jones _____ _____
    Dr. Doe _____ _____

EDUCATION LEVEL OF PATIENT:
    Less than High School_____ _____
    High School _____ _____
    College _____ _____

OCCUPATIONAL LEVEL OF PATIENTS:
    Unemployed _____ _____
    Housewife_____ _____
    Unskilled _____ _____
    Skilled _____ _____
    Self Employed _____ _____
    Clerical _____ _____
    Professional _____ _____
    Student _____ _____
    Disabled_____ _____
    Retired _____ _____

REFERRAL SOURCE OF PATIENTS:
    Self _____ _____
    Former Patient _____ _____
    Physician _____ _____
    Minister _____ _____
    Social Agency _____ _____
    Court _____ _____
    Other Helping Profession _____ _____
    Yellow Pages _____ _____
    Other _____ _____

PAYMENT SOURCE FOR PATIENT:
    Blue Cross _____ _____
    Other Industry Insurance_____ _____
    Medicaid _____ _____
    Private insurance or small group policy _____ _____
    Court _____ _____
    Private Self-Pay _____ _____
    Medicare _____ _____
    V.A. or Champus _____ _____
    Charity _____ _____
    Other _____ _____

TEST ADMINISTERED:
    Yes _____ _____
    No _____ _____

INTAKES THAT SCHEDULED THAT NO SHOWED OR CANCELLED:
    No Showed _____ _____
    Cancelled _____ _____

                TOTAL COMPLETED INTAKES FOR THE MONTH: _____
                                           DATE:_____

List Referring Physicians and Mental Health personnel on back side

SAMPLE 52

INTER-OFFICE FORM

CHECK SHEET
FOR
EFFECTIVE COMMUNICATION

Therapist:_____Date:_____

Patient:_____

You need to take care of the following matter:

We are concerned about the above mentioned case as it relates to **one** or **more** of the areas stated below.

If you have any questions concerning any of the check marks (✓) then please see the receptionist immediately.

We are especially concerned that all material within each file is up-to-date, since we can be audited by private insurance companies and/or governmental agencies at any time.

I. **Intake Sheet:**
_____First Page
_____Second Page
_____Third Page
_____Other Information _____
_____

II. **Therapy Summary Sheet:**
(1) **First Page**
_____General Information
_____Reason for Referral
_____Significant Information
_____Diagnostic Impression (DSM III code and description)
_____Prognostic Impression
_____Termination Information
_____Re-Termination

(2) **Second Page**
_____Type of Therapy
_____Patient Contact

(3) **Third Page, etc.**
_____Patient Contact—Dates to be included:_____,_____,_____,_____,_____.

III. **Hospital Record Sheet:**
_____Date of Visit
_____Patient's Name
_____Time spent with patient or charge
_____Therapy Notes
_____Therapy notes need to be copied onto the regular **Therapy Summary Sheet**

IV. **Communication to Referring Person:**

_____Letter needs to be sent to referring agency

_____Letter needs to be sent to referring physician or person

_____Letter needs to be sent to referring school

_____Letter needs to be sent to referring person_____

_____Phone call needs to be made to the referring agency

_____Phone call needs to be made to the referring physician or person

_____Phone call needs to be made to the referring school

_____Phone call needs to be made to the referring person_____

V. **Securing Additional Information:**

_____Need to obtain medical release form in order to **obtain** needed information

_____Need to obtain social-psychological release form in order to **obtain** needed information

_____Need to obtain office release form in order to **send** information to referring agency, physician, or third party

VI. **Appointments:**

_____Need to fill out the appointment card every week for your patient.

_____Need to fill out our appointment card to verify if the patient was in for the appointment. This way the receptionist can credit you with seeing a patient and help with the problem of scheduling. This card is utilized only for appointments that are scheduled after 5 p.m. and all day Saturday and Sunday—when no receptionist is present in the office.

VII. **Other Category:**

_____ _____
_____
_____
_____

_____ _____
_____
_____
_____

SECTION XI

THE ESSENTIALS

OF A

SUCCESSFUL COLLECTION PROGRAM

NOTES

SECTION XI

THE ESSENTIALS OF A SUCCESSFUL COLLECTION PROGRAM

I. Patient Education

A. Collection can be a very expensive process, but it doesn't have to be. Collecting for services as they are rendered can reduce these costs dramatically. As you know, the cost of collection is eventually passed on from you to the patient—so, to avoid this, **educate your patients.**

B. The first step in **patient education is the phone**. Explain your policy, your charges, and that you expect payment in full on the same day services are rendered.

C. The second step takes place **during intake procedure**. Openly discuss your policy, charges, and the fact that you expect payment in full the same day services are rendered.

D. The third step is to restate everything in your **patient information brochure** and **fee schedule card.** Point out that these points are important for the patients to know and understand and that you will expect them to read them over carefully.

II. Collecting Efficiently From a Peg Board System

If you are on a **peg board system** (which in most cases we recommend), follow the steps listed below. **Sample 31, and 32, pages 104.** It is best to remove page 104 from the binder and place it next to this page for reference while you read the instructions below.

A. When the patient comes in, the receptionist fills in the (sequential) receipt number and date on **service rendered form**-A sample 31, and the previous balance and patient's name on service rendered from-B sample 32. Form-B is then detached and stapled to the patient's folder. When the session is over, the therapist checks the services rendered, notes any special charges, and writes in the patient's next appointment.

B. As soon as the receptionist totals up the charge, **it is time to say the following:**

1. "Hello, Mr. Patient, your **previous balance** was five dollars; today's charges are thirty dollars, making your balance thirty-five dollars. Will this be cash or check?"

2. Pause-wait for a commitment. **The next person to speak loses.**

3. If the excuse is that the patient forgot a checkbook, and does not have a cent on hand, then make the following statement. "Fine, Mr. Patient, here is an envelope with our address on it. Please use this as a reminder to yourself to **write us a check as soon as you get home."**

4. Once the **payment** has been taken care of, the **next appointment** can be set up if required.

III. Collection Tips

A. Use a **charge slip** for each patient visit with a record of the charge for that day's service, plus any previous balance due.

B. Always have the patient take the charge slip to the receptionist **after each session.**

C. **Don't offer to bill the patient**; instead, say, "Your previous balance, Mr. Smith, was $30.00, and today's charge is $15.00. Your total balance due is $45.00. Will this be cash or check?" Wait for the patient to comment. The next person to speak loses.

D. If at all possible, state the fee **before** the services are rendered.

E. **Consistency in your policy**, especially that of collecting cash, is most important.

F. **Never badger or intimidate a patient into paying cash.** Instead, explain your policy and educate. The methods of receiving payment for services rendered, including insurance, should be clearly explained to every patient.

G. The secret of collecting fees is **simply to ask people to pay**. Once again, "Will this be cash or check?"

H. Your **collection percentages** are accurate indicators of the degree to which your patients are being educated.

I. **New patients should pay cash on the first visit**, even if they have been referred to you by another professional. Set a standard for them to follow.

J. Know the age of your accounts; very **old accounts** continue to **cost you money.**

K. The **overhead ratio** can be markedly thrown off if there is an unbalance in collections.

L. Billings should be sent on the same day or days of each month. **Consistency is important**. The 21st, 22nd, and 23rd of the month are good times to mail out.

M. Many accounts over six months old **prove to be uncollectable.**

N. Strive to maintain at least a **95% collection ratio.**

O. Collection letters should be **brief** and **directly** to the **point.**

P. Some offices send out statements **two** to **three days** after services are rendered.

Q. The person or persons collecting money or working overdue accounts **should not** be adverse to doing so.

R. The main advantage of using a **small claims court** is having the **debtor served a summons.** Most patients will make arrangements to pay when they realize you are serious. However, confidentiality "goes out the window" when you take a patient into a small claims court—in return the patient may take you to court for breaking confidentiality of a doctor-patient relationship.

S. The **proper use of the telephone** when working with past due accounts is extremely important.

IV. **Collection Steps—Checklist**

    A. In-office collection attempt.

    B. Early payment envelope.

    C. First statement.

    D. Second statement—30 days late first past due notice.

    E. First phone call—45 days late.

    F. Third statement—60 days late.

    G. Therapist writes a personal note—65 days late.

    H. Second phone call—75 days late.

    I. Fourth statement—90 days late.

    J. Third party letter—100 days late.

    K. Third party (attorney or collection agency) intervention—110 days late.

    L. Dispose of account.

V. **Telephone Collecting**

    A. Before you start, you should acquire basic information such as:

        1. Dates of visits.

        2. Type of treatment rendered.

        3. The amount due.

    B. Gather together all previous collection efforts, such as the following:

        1. Bills (dates).

        2. Calls (dates).

        3. What happened in the past?

    C. Payment history.

        1. How often have they been overdue?

    D. Determine guarantor.

    E. Payment plan minimums.

        1. What payments are acceptable?

2. Dates that payments must be received by.

F. Prepare fact finding questions.

   1. Patient's reason for not paying.

   2. How can you help to bring the account up to date?

G. The call introduction.

   1. Identify yourself and the therapist.

   2. Confrontation—reason for calling.

   3. Wait for response.

   4. Determine problem.

   5. Answer objections.

   6. Work out agreements.

   7. Reiterate commitment.

      (A) review exact amount.
      (B) review exact dates due.
      (C) record.
      (D) file for automatic review.

H. Follow up.

   1. Review progress.

   2. Action.

      (A) refile in follow-up accounts.
      (B) refile in open accounts.
      (C) continue collection process.

VI. Telephone Objections

A. Payment is in the mail.

Answer: When was it sent?
From where was it sent?
How much was sent?
Why was it late?

B. Out of work or illness.

Answer: Why?
How long?
Are you receiving unemployment compensation or sick leave compensation?
Prospects of returning to work?
Why didn't you let us know?
Is spouse working?

C. **Separation or divorce.**

Answer: Date.
Attorneys (both parties).
His and her employer.
Advise debtor of liability.
If debtor will not commit, find out why.
Secure address and phone of separated spouse.
Set future date for next contact.

D. **Bankruptcy.**

Answer: Obtain date and number.
If secured, explain rights.
If unsecured, explain loss of services.
Check for fraud.
Stop collection efforts.

E. **Death of debtor.**

Answer: Date and place of death.
Name and address of administrator.
Name and address of attorney.
File creditor claim.

F. **Determining payment potential.**

Answer: If payment can be made, establish amount and date expected.
If payment cannot be made:
1. agree to moratorium, if indicated;
2. require continuous phone contact;
3. control future services;
4. review account bi-weekly.

VII. **Motivating Statements For Telephone Collection**

A. Have you **mailed a check** to the therapist yet?

B. In order to keep your account current, we will **need payment this week.**

C. I will go over unpaid accounts with the therapist on Friday, I would like to have **your check before then.**

D. Our policy requires **all accounts** to be kept on a current basis. We need your check this afternoon. Is it possible?

E. If the account remains unpaid, it will be **referred to our Attorney**. If you do not want this to happen, you must mail your check now.

F. The **collection agency** picks up all **our delinquent accounts** this Friday . . . I know you don't want your account included . . . can you send someone in with a check today?

VIII. **Authorizations**

A. **Third party authorizations** allow you to avoid what is known as the ping pong effect **(Samples 53-54 on pages 158-159)**. Until you have this signed and returned to you, make the person bringing in the patient responsible.

IX. **Skiptracing**

A. This is directed to professional offices; that is, to the time and tools normally available to the assistant in a typical clinic office. Most of the work will be done by phone, not mail. For starters, we will point out that the purpose of skiptracing is to **locate assets** that will **help us to collect**. Just getting information is a waste of time once we determine that collection is unlikely, anyway. But, how do you know, ahead of time, when it is unproductive to skiptrace for a patient who has skipped? Here are three good reasons not to waste your time:

1. Patient's **past record** indicates no payment possiblities.

2. The **size of the account** does not warrant much effort.

3. Past tracing efforts **never resulted** in collection.

B. If you can **categorize your patient** from his or her habits and attitude, you will have more guidance as to the likelihood of payment, assuming you locate the person. Here, then, is a review of common debtor types:

1. **Patient with good intentions** —thinks he or she is honest, but won't make the first move. Usually collectable accounts.

2. **Self-righteous patients** —had to sit in your waiting room for an hour, or maybe you did not help them to an expected level of satisfaction. May be a problem collecting.

3. **Procrastinators** —will pay, but time is not important to them.

4. **Poor planners** —a miracle will happen. Life will get better. Has no reserve to fall back on. Collecting may involve financial counseling as well as waiting.

5. **Irresponsible patients** —may be respected, honest, citizens, but are financially immature. But until they are in serious financial difficulty it may be difficult to collect from them.

6. **Stallers** —they buy time. "You didn't get my check? I'll put a tracer on it." (But that will take a few weeks and no check was sent anyway)—or, "I didn't get full credit for my payment" (so now you have to check that out). Their delaying tactics can wear you down.

7. **Indigents** —honest, but cannot pay. Uncollectable.

8. **Chronic debtors** —collection letters and phone calls are a way of life to them. Uncollectable.

9. **Credit criminals** —who set out intentionally to defraud their creditors. Uncollectable.

C. Now that we have some idea of who not to bother skiptracing for, we now need to know, for those who may be collectable if found, what **information we should develop.**

1. **Patient's name** —be sure to get middle name or initial and whether patient is junior or senior.

2. **Correct address**—including zip code. Also, check for former address, as this can provide some good leads.

3. **Employer**—type of work or trade is important. Many people have to register with the state, no matter what city they are in, e.g. barbers, private investigators, collectors. Members of trade unions, school teachers, nurses, etc., are fairly easy to locate once you find the area they have skipped to. In the case of single people living at home, get employment address of parents. If you have only a former employer, ask where the W-2 form was sent.

4. **Real estate**—does patient rent, lease or own property? If he or she owns, who is the mortgager? What insurance broker handled the home insurance? If the patient is a renter, obtain landlord's name and address.

5. **Personal property**—for a car, who is the legal owner? If patient belongs to a credit union, it is likely that assets would be listed on the loan application.

6. **Neighbors and friends**—neighbors are an excellent source of data on a skip. What moving company came for the furniture? Does the neighbor know any of the skip's friends or relatives? Where did he or she work?

D. Since we now know what information we want, the next steps are to **learn where to get the information and how to get it.** First, where do we get information for skip-tracing? Bear in mind that hospitals will use more tools than these and collection agencies will still use more, but the cost of some skiptracing tools puts them well beyond the economic justification of most therapists.

1. **Telephone**—the best single tool.

2. **City directory**—available in the public library. Includes a listing of business and professional firms, an alphabetic list of names of residents and businesses in the community, including spouses, marital status, occupation and address. Also includes a numerical phone listing, which enables you to find the name of the person who has a given phone number. Also lists householders by street and avenue, showing occupant, whether or not residence is owned, and phone number.

3. **Criss-Cross telephone directory**—also available in the public library. This directory lists numbered and then alphabetical streets. On each street, the house numbers are arranged in numerical order, showing name of occupant or business and the telephone number. Great for talking to neighbors.

4. **Miscellaneous**—includes church directory, high school directories of seniors, chamber of commerce directories on businesses, social security number (for $1.00 they will tell you who is paying into that number), board of education directory, military base directory, driver's license, etc.

E. The following are **some techniques for skiptracing** on the phone. First of all, be friendly. You are asking for help from someone who does not know you. The person may be busy. And no one wants to be an informer. You need to let the person think he or she is helping you and not hurting the patient. The steps in your call are these:

1. **Identify the informant**—"Is this Mrs. John Williams at 310 North Main Street?"

2. **Identify yourself**—"Mrs. Williams, this is Bill Smith."

3. **State the problem** —"I need to get in touch with Joe Patient."

4. **Ask for help** —"Can you help me?"

5. **Then listen**. Listen for attitude and for leads. Ask questions: "Do you know where he is?" "Do you know who else can help me?"

6. **People love to correct you**. If you want to know where Joe Patient works, ask, "Does Joe still work at General Electric?" If you simply ask where Joe works, it sounds as though you don't know Joe at all, and information will not follow so quickly.

7. Be prepared for **two key questions** by informant:

   (A) "Who did you say this was?" Answer: "A friend," and then go right into another question.

   (B) "What do you want him for?" Answer: Several possible answers, such as "Well, it's sort of a surprise, and I'd really appreciate your help in reaching him."

8. Also, **convey a sense of urgency** —"I've just got to get in touch with Joe."

9. When dealing **with businesses, use the direct approach**. This includes banks, former employers, utilities, and other businesses. State that you are skiptracing: you will usually get full cooperation.

10. Another idea is to **write down phone numbers commonly used** in skiptracing, such as library, assessor's office, and phone company.

11. Phone operators are busy on weekdays. They will be much more eager to search for you if you **call during slack times**, such as on Saturday.

F. **Some final words**: If you do not have time for skiptracing, get the account right into collection. If you do attempt to skiptrace, but you do not succeed, also assign those accounts for collection. Of the accounts received for collection, 35%-50% are skips. This means that collection agencies have a lot more expertise in tracing, so they often find people that you cannot.

Skiptracing can be as challenging as detective work. If only you had more time! You can at least try the neighbors, which will increase your chances of collecting yourself.

X. Utilizing a Collection Agency

A. Many practitioners absolutely refuse to turn a patient over to a collection agency, or to use a small claims court themselves. Between the two, the **collection agency is the best tool.** The following explanation will help you understand why. If you use the court systems yourself to collect bad debts from patients, you open yourself up to the possibility of a law suit by the patient against you. Why? Because by using this system yourself there is a chance that your local newspaper might pick up on the suit and print it for everyone to read! Dr. John Doe versus Joe Patient in the paper has just revealed to the world that Joe Patient has been seeing a shrink! Joe Patient, if he is sharp, will then turn around and sue you for **breaching his confidentiality**. On the other hand, if you had turned that same patient over to a professional collection agency, there might not have been a summons served because there is a good chance that the agency would collect what you couldn't and even if they had to take your patient to court to collect, it would have read in the local newspaper like this: Allied Collection Agency versus Joe Patient.

B. Of all accounts that are turned over to collection agencies, **35% to 50% are called skips**: people who have moved, leaving no forwarding address and no other traces for you to find them. However, **collection agencies have the expertise to skiptrace**, and can usually find this type of person.

C. **Remember this**: select your collection agency as you would your banker. Both of them are entrusted with your money! Here is a list of priorities to help you select the right collection agency:

1. Look for **integrity** within the agency.

2. Make sure the agency is **affiliated** with other collection agencies all over the country.

3. **Talk to** some of the agency's **larger clients** about how it has handled their accounts.

4. If at all possible, do your business **with a local agency.**

5. Take into consideration the agency's **fee basis**. Most agencies will be competitive within the same area. Shop around.

6. Stay away from **graduated fee scales**. These are known as "cream skimmers" in the collection business.

7. The agency you choose should at least be **licensed with the state**, and should preferably belong to a state and/or a national association, such as the American Collection Association.

8. Be able to get a **5 to 10 days grace period on collections** from your agency. Example: if you turn the account over to an agency, and the patient immediately pays the bill because of this action, you should get 100% of the paid bill.

9. **Be able to take the account back**. Be sure to check the local law on this; you may not legally be able to do so.

10. The **national average** of collection among agencies **is 38%**. If your agency is doing less than that, change to another agency with a better average.

11. If the collection agency is harassing your patient, **YOU ARE DIRECTLY INVOLVED!** A collection agency should have a strict policy about this, especially when the individual is a patient of a professional. If a collector hears a patient mention the word sue, court action, etc. he or she should stop all collection efforts immediately on your behalf.

12. **Don't be afraid to use a collection agency**. Remember: 50% collection on a bad debt is better than 100% of nothing.

SAMPLE 53

THIRD PARTY AUTHORIZATION

**THIRD PARTY AUTHORIZATION
FORM**

_____, one of my
patients, has informed me that you intend to assume the financial obligation for charges
he/she incurs at this office. You must agree to keep the balance paid in full. In order to verify
this fact, I would appreciate your signature at the bottom of this form. Please return as soon
as possible for our files.

Sincerely yours,

_____
John Doe, Ph.D.
Psychologist

I, _____, the undersigned, do
promise to pay the expenses rendered by Dr. John Doe for the above named patient.

Date:_____ Signature: _____

This form could be utilized with a bank trust department, a guardian or responsible (financial)
parent when divorced or anyone else who would be responsible for the payment of psychotherapy—other than self-pay or insurance.

SAMPLE 54

AUTHORIZATION TO PAY PSYCHOLOGIST

To be completed by the insured employee for direct pay to the Psychologist.

I hereby authorize payment to _____
                                            Name of Psychologist

of the Group Medical Insurance Expense otherwise payable to me, but not to exceed the fees stated for these services. I understand I am financially responsible to the psychologist for charges not covered by this authorization.

Date:_____ Signed:_____
                                            (Insured Employee)

This form can be utilized by the psychologist when submitting an insurance claim for services rendered—especially, if the insurance form does not properly indicate if the payment should be sent to the patient or the provider of the service.

NOTES

SECTION XII

THIRD PARTY REIMBURSEMENT

NOTES

SECTION XII

THIRD PARTY REIMBURSEMENT

PRIVATE INSURANCE

I. Historical Perspective

A. Historically, coverage by third parties at best has been limited for **mental and nervous (M & N) conditions**. Care for mental illness was not something to be discussed nor acknowledged; and consequently, few employees saw fit in the 40s and 50s to include mental illness benefits in their health care packages.

As time passed, and more care moved from state or other governmental units, and as mental illness became less of a stigma and more of a recognized illness, benefits began to expand. The word "expand" may not seem appropriate in light of the still-limited coverages, but by comparison to what coverages existed even 10 years ago, there has been expansion.

B. Before criticizing third parties for their role in limiting benefits, there are **these factors to consider:**

1. **Lack of buyer initiative**, or awareness for the need of this benefit.

2. **Public apprehension** in admitting the presence of mental illness.

3. Lack of specific and uniform licensing and/or certification **legislation for providers.**

4. Difficulty in actually **predicting** the **costs.**

C. As you can imagine, insurance companies must provide coverage for benefits that the accounts either require or can afford. **No one can provide a benefit for free.**

D. The past thirty years have seen health care coverage expand from a basic thirty day hospital stay to every conceivable form of care. But in this expansion of benefits has come an **increased cost to buyers**, to the purchaser of goods or services of that buyer, and in taxes.

E. In spending their dollars, buyers have continued to add the benefits needed by the majority of their employees and to increase their current benefits to a level meeting their employees' needs. Consequently, the **evolution of adequate mental illness coverage has been slow.**

F. Let's look at **third party** (non-governmental) **involvement** with you as a private practicing professional. In doing so, we will cover the following areas:

1. Who are they?

2. Claim forms.

3. Reimbursement.

4. Benefits.

II. "Who Are These Guys?"

A. **Survey** your own backyard.

B. Contact local **business** and **factory** personnel departments.

C. Ask who their **insurance carriers** are and the nearest office location.

D. Ask for an **abstract** of their benefits.

E. If possible, discuss with the employer any specific coverage or non-coverage of **benefits for mental illness.**

III. Contact The Insurer . . . Easier Than You Think

A. Most major insurers **are eager to discuss** their account's coverage with providers.

B. They probably do not know **you** exist.

C. Be prepared to **lobby** on behalf of yourself and your profession.

D. Be able to **inform** the company as to who you are (name, location, license, proximity to their insured, and what services you are offering).

E. Establish a **liaison** to ease your present relationship and to enhance the future.

IV. Commercials

A. The major commercial (non Blue Cross and Blue Shield) companies have **local** or **regional** claims office.

B. The **claims manager** is normally the person to contact.

C. **Health Insurance Association of America** (HIAA) represents over 300 of the commercial health insurers.

D. HIAA is organized to **coordinate** and **assist providers** and **consumers** in the complaints or problems with their members.

E. HIAA requests **that the problem be resolved** with the individual company, if possible. If not, then contact HIAA.

F. Each state has an **HIAA representative** whom you can contact.

V. Blue Cross and Blue Shield

A. There are 71 plans **nationally. (Sample 55, page 183)**

B. Some states have **one plan**, whereas others may **have more.**

C. **Professional Relations** staffs are available to assist providers.

D. Most have area representatives available to **come to your office**, if necessary.

VI. More Paperwork

A. **Claim forms** are a necessary evil. They must be filed in order for your patient to receive the benefits to which he or she is entitled.

B. They are **not** that **complicated.**

C. They come in **many forms** and **styles**:

1. American Medical Association Uniform Claim Form **(Sample 55, page 183) is accepted** by most third parties.

2. Some insurers do **have special forms** which are often easier to use and require a minimum of information.

3. Find out early what **forms need to be used** and where to obtain them.

   (A) Some companies supply the forms to the provider.

   (B) Some companies require the employee to supply the form to the provider.

4. Check with **all insurers** as to where the claim forms are sent and their position regarding confidentiality.

   (A) Most forms are sent directly to the insurer.

   (B) Some forms must be returned to the employer.

D. **Information is Basically the Same**

1. Patient's name, (DO NOT USE NICKNAMES—*CLARIFY* STEP-CHILDREN, etc., WITH DIFFERENT LAST NAMES).

2. Policy holder's name and address.

3. Identifying numbers—usually one ID number with a possibility of one or more additional numbers which may identify employer, benefits, etc.

4. Patient's age, date of birth, relationship to policy holder, and sex.

5. Patient's signature for release of information (not always needed).

6. Date(s) of services performed.

7. Description of service(s) performed (codes may often be used).

8. Charge(s) for each service.

9. Diagnosis or description of illness (codes may often be used).

10. Signature of provider.

11. Address and either a provider code or social security number.

VII. **Money . . . How Did They Figure That?**

A. Different **types** of reimbursement programs.

1. **Indemnity**—an insurance term indicating a fixed, pre-established level of payment. Has no relativity to the charge . . . can vary greatly . . . is designed to assist the patient in paying his or her bill . . . is not designed to pay the bill in full.

2. **Usual, Customary or Reasonable (UCR)**—a flexible method of reimbursement based upon YOUR (usual) charges as they relate to those of your PEERS (customary). Normally calculated to pay in full the majority of charges from providers.

   (A) Usual

   (B) Customary

   (C) Reasonable

3. **Percent of UCR**—same as item 2, but pays only a percentage (80%, 90%) with the patient responsible for the co-insurance (10%, 20%).

4. **Deductible and Co-Insurance**—usually in the form of major medical type policies. The patient must pay for the first specified dollar amount ($50, $100, $200) and then a percentage of the rest (10%, 20%, 50%).

   (A) The policy often will deduct the first $100 and pay 80% of the remaining charges.

   (B) This is usually for bills in each one year period.

   (C) Some policies have a deductible of services, i.e., they will begin paying after the third visit.

   (D) Some policies apply a co-insurance amount after a number of services, i.e., first 10 visits paid in full, second 10 visits will be paid at 80%, third 10 visits will be paid at 50%, etc.

5. Many policies using any of the above reimbursement methods have **a maximum amount to be paid** per year, per spell of illness or per lifetime.

VIII. **Benefits, Where Are They?**

A. **Major Medical**—currently the most common type of policy covering services of a psychologist.

1. **Deductible and Co-Insurance**—many policies reimburse a lower percentage for mental and nervous conditions than other medical conditions, i.e., 50% vs. 80%, 75%, vs. 90%, etc.

2. The **patient** is normally **expected to file** this type of claim.

   (A) May file itemized billings.

   (B) May file paid statements.

(C) Often, you may file after obtaining an assignment of benefits authorization from the patient—this may be practical if the patient has a large bill and is financially distressed.

3. This type of policy can supplement a basic **first dollar** type of policy or stand alone.

4. Variations of benefits run from testing to therapy and must be ascertained for **each type of policy.**

B. **Basic for first dollar coverage**—this type of policy normally covers benefits without deductibles and an allowance to be applied towards the initial claim or services.

C. Types of benefits can vary under each policy and **should be investigated** prior to rendering services. Doing this will assist your patients in relieving any concerns they may have regarding finances. With these questions clarified initially, treatment should progress more smoothly.

1. Psychological testing.

(A) It is frequently covered.

(B) It is usually indemnified or maximums in either number and/or dollar amounts.

(C) Frequently, policies indicate the testing must be prescribed by a physician.

2. Therapy or Counseling.

(A) Frequently it is only covered if performed by a physician.

(B) It can be covered only for the time necessary for evaluation and diagnosis of mental deficiency or retardation.

(C) It might be covered only for conditions which, according to generally accepted professional standards, are amenable to favorable modification.

(D) It is normally limited to services for emotional and personality disorders and illnesses which are classified as such in the **Eighth Revision, International Classification of Diseases.**

(E) "Milieu" therapy is normally not covered.

D. Benefits by **type** of practice.

1. **Sole practice**—limited benefit availability under most policies. Dependent upon each policy, state and services.

2. **Clinic**—more benefit availability under many policies.

3. **Hospital**—greatest benefit availability. In patient services by employees of the facility normally covered. Greater problem with coverage for admission and continued stays.

MEDICAID

I. Historical Perspective

A. **Medicaid** was established under Title XIX of the Social Security Act of 1965.

    1. Medicaid is a **Federal-State Program** which is designed to provide medical assistance to those groups or categories of people who are eligible to receive payments under one of the existing welfare programs established under the Social Security Act—Title IV, Aid to Families with Dependent Children (AFDC), or the Supplemental Security Income Program (SSI) for the aged, blind, and disabled.

    2. States also may provide coverage to the **medically needy.** This includes people who fit into one of the above categories and have sufficient income for their living expenses, but not enough to pay for their medical care.

B. The program is administered by each **State** with broad **Federal guidelines**, and there are wide variations in coverages with federal contributions ranging from 50-78%.

    1. There are only **eight services** which must be offered to meet cost sharing requirements.

        (A) In-patient hospital card.

        (B) Outpatient hospital services.

        (C) Laboratory and X-ray services.

        (D) Skilled nursing facility services.

        (E) Home health services for persons 21 and older.

        (F) Early and Periodic screening, diagnosis and treatment for persons under 21.

        (G) Family planning.

        (H) Physicians' services (generally considered to include only those physicians with an unlimited license to practice Medicine—M.D. or D.O.).

    2. **Early and Periodic Screening, Diagnosis and Treatment (EPSDT)** was legislated by the U.S. Congress as a required preventive health service to be covered by the Medicaid Program. EPSDT is to be made available to all persons under the age of 21 who are certified for Medicaid. The full cooperation of Medicaid providers is necessary to administer this portion of Medicaid.

    3. The purpose of EPSDT is to direct the attention of recipient parents and youth to the importance of **preventive health examinations** (health screenings) and the need for obtaining necessary follow-up medical care and treatment as prescribed for conditions which are discovered through these health screenings.

    The entrance to EPSDT is through the acceptance of eligible children and youth by a physician or clinic for health screening.

    The health screening procedure, at a minimum, is to include attention to each child's vision, hearing, dental condition, and general physical and mental health.

Unless appropriate diagnosis and follow-up care and treatment, as may be indicated by the results of health screening, are provided, the purpose of the program will be defeated. It is vitally essential that his loss in health effort not be permitted to happen under the EPSDT program.

4. A **chart** showing Medicaid services **state-by-state** is available from Health, Education and Welfare or the proper agency in your state.

5. This chart does not specifically relate to services rendered by psychologists. Whereas psychologists' services are covered in some states, the best advice at this point would be to **contact the proper agency in your state.**

II. Eight Basic Services

A. Even though there are **eight basic services**, there may be limitations on the manner in which states may authorize services, the number of services, or other standards at the election of the state agency.

1. For example, some states may have **no limitations**, while another may require **prior authorization** for psychiatric treatment when costs exceed $300 in a given year.

2. Some states **may impose cost sharing requirements** (co-payments) on optional services for each assistance recipients and on any services for the medically needy. However, as a result of P.L. 92-603 (1972 Social Security Amendments), no cost sharing can be imposed on the mandatory services for cash assistance recipients.

III. Reimbursement

A. Another variable which enters into the picture is the **method of reimbursement**. Some states reimburse on a fixed fee schedule, some on a negotiated fee, while others utilize a usual, customary and reasonable fee schedule. Therefore, they vary widely in terms of reimbursement for physicians' services in the different states.

1. Except for in-patient hospital services which are to be reimbursed on the basis of reasonable cost, there is no requirement for Medicaid reimbursement other than State Medicaid reimbursement which may not exceed the amounts paid under Medicare.

2. Medicaid operates as a vendor payment program which provides payment directly to the provider of service.

3. Providers participating must accept the Medicaid reimbursement level as payment in full.

B. Many persons are **covered by both Medicare and Medicaid**. The states may enroll and make the monthly premium for Medicare Part B. These "buy in" agreements between the State Medicaid Program and the Social Security Program allow eligibility for some who might not be able to afford to pay the premiums themselves. Under this arrangement, Medicare makes the primary payment for the service, and Medicaid is limited to the deductible and co-payment.

C. Medicaid is a **last pay** program. Coverage is available only for that portion which is in excess of other health, accident, or other insurance coverage.

D. **Inquiries** should be made into **all such policies or benefits**, including the circumstances giving rise to the need for benefits, and to determine the availability of Workmen's Compensation coverage as most states will withhold actual medicaid liability. Other insurance payments will be deducted from the Medicaid payment.

IV. Psychological Services

A. As stated earlier, psychologists' services may be covered in some states and not others. As with Medicare, coverage may be **limited to testing or incident to services,** while others may be very inclusive covering psychotherapy, etc.

B. Many of the states provide coverage for services provided by an **Outpatient Mental Health Center or Clinic**. As an example, one state provides coverage for group and individual outpatient psychotherapy, psychiatric testing, evaluations, and psychological testing, and evaluations to an outpatient mental health clinic which has available the services of a psychiatrist, psychologist, and ACSW social workers.

C. In this particular example, some **very strict parameters** are established.

1. The **psychiatrist bears the responsiblity** for establishing the diagnosis and treatment plan and for supervising the execution of that treatment plan. The psychiatrist is responsible for seeing the recipient during the intake process and again at intervals not to exceed six months. The psychiatrist must be available to see patients when emergencies arise and when the staff requests additional consultation. The psychiatrist should be identified as a part of the on-site staff with responsibility for all clinical functions. The psychiatrist should be on duty, on-site, a sufficient amount of time to discharge his or her responsibilities adequately and regularly.

2. Claims submitted by an outpatient psychiatric clinic for services rendered by a psychologist must include a copy of the **physician's referral statement or a copy of the psychiatrist's treatment plan** for claims processing. When psychotherapy is provided by an ACSW social worker, a copy of the psychiatrist's treatment plan, including diagnosis, length of treatment, and type of therapy are required for each claim submitted.

V. Diagnostic Evaluation

A. The diagnosis or illness must be found in the section of **Diagnostic Nomenclature** of the **Diagnostic and Statistical Manual of Mental Disorders** published by the American Psychiatric Association. Psychiatric and psychological evaluation and testing are covered services and are reimbursable for all diagnoses. Reimbursement for psychotherapy will be made for all diagnoses except the following:

1. The category of Transient Situation Disturbance.

2. The category of Social Maladjustments without manifest psychiatric disorder.

3. The category of non-specific conditions.

4. The category of no mental disorder.

VI. Claim Submission

A. The information required for claim submission may vary, too. However, this information is becoming more and more standardized with the implementation of the **Medicaid Management Information System (MMIS)**.

1. **Another aspect of the 1972 Social Security Amendments** was the authorization of 90% federal matching to states for the costs of design, development and installation of mechanized claims processing and information retrieval systems and 75% ongoing for the cost of operating the systems. MMIS was a model system developed by the Department of Health, Education, and Welfare. At this point, almost all of the states have implemented, are implementing, or are planning on implementing it.

2. The **Medicaid claim** form example does not contain MMIS date elements but does contain the information needed for processing. **Sample 56, page 184.**

3. Information such as these items **will be needed:**

   (A) **Patient Name** —this must coincide with the recipient's identification card.

   (B) **Medicaid Number** —show this number exactly as it appears on the recipient's ID card. Note that each member of a family has a unique number.

   (C) **Patient's Address** —if patient is residing in a nursing home, indicate the nursing home's name and address.

   (D) **Patient's Date of Birth** —should coincide with identification card.

   (E) **Patient Referral** —indicate name and provider number of referring practitioner.

   (F) Note whether or not the patient was involved in an **accident or if the patient's illness or injury was connected with his or her job.**

   (G) Record whether or not the recipient has **other health insurance** which will pay part of his or her medical expenses.

   (H) **Primary and Secondary diagnosis** —enter the primary and secondary diagnosis and/or the code.

   (I) **Date of Service** —indicate the date that services were provided.

   (J) **Description of Surgical or Medical Procedures and Other Services or Supplies** —describe fully the types of service which were actually rendered.

   (K) **Family Planning.**

   (L) **Place of Service** —a complete itemization of charges is required, i.e., charge for each office call.

   (M) **Less Amount Received from Other Sources** —indicate the amount paid by the patient or by other resources on the patient's behalf.

   (N) **Billing Date** —indicate the month, day, and year the claim is being submitted.

   (O) **Signature of Provider** —the provider of service must sign his or her name or use a signature stamp to certify that services were performed as stated.

   (P) **Early Periodic Screening Diagnosis and Treatment (EPSDT).**

4. Again, the key to submitting claims properly, efficiently, and at a maximum reimbursement under the program begins **with a contact to the State or Fiscal Agent.**

MEDICARE

I. Historical Perspective

A. The **Medicare Program** is a federal health insurance program established by an act of Congress (Title XVIII of the Social Security Act in 1965).

1. This program is **administered through carriers and intermediaries** at the direction of the Medicare Bureau, Health Care Financing Administration, which is under the Secretary of the Department of Health, Education, and Welfare.

2. There are **two distinct parts** to the Medicare Program: **Hospital Insurance** (Part A) and **Supplementary Medical Insurance** (Part B). Hospital Insurance (Part A) is available to nearly everyone 65 or over. Effective July, 1973, two additional groups of individuals became eligible for participation. Disabled workers, disabled children, disabled mothers, and disabled widows and widowers who have been entitled to monthly cash disability benefits for 24 consecutive months comprise the first group. The second is comprised of individuals requiring hemodialysis or renal transplantation for chronic renal disease. Eligibility for chronic renal disease beneficiaries begins with the third month after the month in which a course of renal hemodialysis begins and continues through the 12th month after the month in which an individual has a successful transplant or dialysis terminates. Supplementary Medical insurance (Part B) is voluntary and, though in most cases the beneficiary does enroll, he or she may decline if he or she so wishes.

II. Coverage for Psychological Services

A. The **only coverage available** under the Medicare Program for the services of a qualified independent psychologist is for psychological testing if a physician orders such testing.

1. **A qualified psychologist is an individual who, if practicing in a state where statutory licensure or certification exists, holds a valid credential as legally specified for such practice.**. If the state has no licensure or certification, the psychology from an American Psychological Association approved program in clinical psychology or its adjudged equivalent, or have attained recognition of competency through the American Board of Examination for Professional Psychology or through endorsement by his or her state psychological association.

2. A psychologist would be considered as **practicing independently** where:

(A) The psychologist renders services on his or her responsibility, **free of the administration and professional control of an employer**, such as a physician, institution, agency, etc.

(B) The persons the psychologist treats are his or her **own patients**, and;

(C) The psychologist **has the right** to bill directly for, collect, and retain the fee for his or her services.

3. A psychologist practicing in an office located in an institution may be considered

an independently practicing psychologist when both of the **two conditions below are met:**

(A) The office must be confined to a separately identified part of the facility which is **used solely** as the psychologist's office and cannot be construed as extending throughout the entire institution; and

(B) **Carries on a private practice**, i.e., services are rendered to patients from outside the institution as well as to institutional patients.

III. Diagnostic Testing

A. Manual instructions require that the **name and address** of the physician ordering the diagnostic tests be indicated on the claim form.

1. The physician ordering the tests should be the **attending physician or consulting physician.**

2. It is of prime importance that the ordering physician will have had **recent contact with the beneficiary and should have some basis for indicating why the diagnostic psychological testing is necessary** (what is he or she attempting to confirm or rule out? The Medicare Program does not provide coverage for screening examination or services). Therefore, there should be a specific order by the physician giving the psychologist adequate information regarding the condition the physician is seeking to assess. Of course, the various psychological tests administered should be related to the diagnosis indicated on the claim form.

IV. Reimbursement

A. Reimbursement for diagnostic psychological services performed by qualified independent psychologists will be made on the basis of the **reasonable charge as determined by the carrier**. Expenses for such testing are not subject to the payment limitations on treatment for mental, psychoneurotic, and personality disorders. The psychologist may accept assignment under the usual procedures or may bill the patient who will then seek reimbursement from the program.

1. The **time involved in the psychologist's service** will be the principal factor when determining the reasonable charge where the psychologist ordinarily bills on a time-unit basis. Thus, where the bill is based on the number and length of sessions involved, the psychologist's customary half-hour and hourly rates, and prevailing half-hour and hourly rates for psychologists' services in the locality should be used in making the reasonable charge determinations.

(A) The **time expended by a psychologist in the preparation of the report** is to be considered an intergral part of the diagnostic testing service and not a separately covered service.

(B) If the psychologist customarily bases his or her fee on **factors other than time**, the usual criteria for the determination of reasonable charges will be applied to the specific diagnostic procedure performed.

2. **Medicare allowances are based upon a usual and customary concept**. To determine Medicare reimbursement, profiles are developed by using actual charges submitted by suppliers for Medicare beneficiaries. The profiles are calculated in accordance with the rules and regulations from the Department of Health, Education, and Welfare, Social Security Administration. Medicare regulations re-

quire that the reasonable charge recognized for any particular service must be the lowest of: (a) the supplier's **usual charge** for the service; (b) the **customary** or **prevailing charge** made for similar services by other suppliers in the locality; or (c) the **actual charge** made on the claim by the supplier. As early as possible at the beginning of each fee screen year (the 12 month period beginning in July), Medicare compiles the fee information collected during the **previous** full calendar year to develop **new** Medicare allowances. In this manner, the reasonable charge allowances are updated annually to reflect the changes in supplier charge patterns. Since this updating is done annually, Medicare cannot immediately respond with a higher allowance at the time of a individual supplier's fee increase. Furthermore, as shown below, the customary charge determination tends to reflect the supplier's most frequently charged fee for a service and not necessarily the highest or most current fee.

(A) **The Usual Charge** — A supplier's usual charge is determined to be that amount which best represents the actual charges made for a given service by a supplier to his or her patient in general. In calculating the usual charge for a given procedure, each charge the supplier has made for that service during the previous calendar year is arrayed in ascending order. The lowest actual charge which is high enough to include the median (middle charge) is selected as the usual charge. However, a supplier must have performed a given procedure a minimum of three (3) times during the preceding year for Medicare beneficiaries before a usual charge determination is made. For example, assume that the figures below represent the charges made by a supplier for a particular procedure that was performer twelve times during the year.

EXAMPLE OF USUAL CHARGE CALCULATION

Charges	Frequency	Cumulative Services
$24.00	2	2
25.00	2	4
26.00	4	8—Median
27.00	4	12

The median charge is the charge at which one half of the charges fall above or below. In this example, the median is the 6th charge. The lowest charge high enough to include the median is $26.00 and this amount will be recognized as the supplier's usual charge for this particular purpose.

(B) **The Customary or Prevailing Charge** — From the calculated usual charges, the customary or prevailing allowance determination is made for each specialty by locality. At least four (4) suppliers in the same specialty and locality must have a calculated usual charge for a given procedure before a prevailing charge can be established for that procedure. The prevailing charge for each medical service is then established at the 75th percentile of the calculated charges weighted by frequency of service. The intent is to establish a level of reimbursement which is high enough to cover in full the customary charges of those suppliers whose billings accounted for at least 75 percent of all claims for that service in the locality in the preceding calendar year. For a simplified illustration of this calculation, assume that suppliers established the usual charges and frequencies of service noted below:

EXAMPLE OF USUAL CHARGE CALCULATION

Usual Charge	Number of Services rendered by Suppliers with usual charges as indicated	Cumulative Services
$25.00	100	100
$26.00	300	400
$27.00—75th percentile	350	750
$28.00	250	1000

75% x 1000 equal 750

The 750th service in the "array" falls in the $27.00 charge range. In this example Medicare must determine a prevailing charge that will be high enough to cover at least 75% of the services rendered. Seventy-five percent of the total of 1000 services equals 750 services. The prevailing charge is, therefore, $27.00, as $27.00 will be high enough to cover 75% (or more) of the services rendered. The above explains the underlying basis for the profile determination for the Medicare Program.

B. **Deductible** —In each calendar year, the patient must satisfy a deductible of $60.00 before Medicare payment can be made. The total reasonable charge allowance on a claim is reduced by the amount of any remaining deductible prior to payment. Bills count toward the deductible on the basis of incurred rather than paid expenses. **Non-covered expenses do not count toward the deductible**. Expenses incurred in the last three months of a year, **which were applied toward the medical insurance deductible for that year**, also may be applied against the deductible for the next year. This is called the "carryover" provision. The date of service generally determines when expenses were incurred, but expenses are allocated to the deductible in the order in which the bills are received by Medicare. An adjustment will be made, however, when expenses incurred in the fourth quarter of one year are used to satisfy the deductible for the following year and it is subsequently determined that the patient has incurred covered expenses prior to the fourth quarter of the earlier year. Even though an individual who is recently covered under Medicare may not have been eligible for payments during the entire calendar year, he or she is still required to satisfy the full $60.00 deductible.

C. **Co-Insurance** —For psychology services, Medicare pays 80% of the reasonable charge, after subtracting any remaining deductible.

D. **The Assignment Agreement** —Under the Medicare law, acceptance of an assignment requires the physician or supplier to accept the carrier's determination of the allowable charge for a service as his or her full charge for that service. This means that for services covered under an assignment agreement, the physician or supplier cannot bill the patient for more than the difference between the allowable charge determined by the carrier and the payment received from the carrier. The beneficiary is still responsible to the physician or supplier of service and may be billed for the Medicare co-insurance (20%) and any portion of the $60.00 Medicare deductible. In addition, the beneficiary, is responsible and may be billed for any services which are non-covered for any reason other than a reasonable charge reduction in the Medicare allowance. Payment cannot be demanded from the beneficiary in assignment cases for the difference between the allowable charge and the actual charge, if a reduction of the actual charge has been made by the Medicare carrier. An assignment agreement, once made, cannot be revoked in whole or in part by one party alone without a consent of the other party.

E. Time Limits for filing Part B Medicare Claims

FOR SERVICES RECEIVED	CLAIMS MUST BE FILED BY
October 1, 1981-September 30, 1982	December 31, 1983
October 1, 1982-September 30, 1983	December 31, 1984
October 1, 1983-September 30, 1984	December 31, 1985
October 1, 1984-September 30, 1985	December 31, 1986

These established limits for filing may be waived if it is determined that through an error or delay on the part of SSA or the carrier (administrative error), the claimant failed to file within the time limitation.

F. There is **no provision in the Medicare law** that covers psychotherapy services rendered by independently practicing non-physician medical personnel (e.g., psychologist and psychiatric social worker), or those psychologists on the staff of a free-standing clinic which is not physician directed.

1. However, the **therapeutic** (i.e., psychotherapy) and **social work services** (as distinguished from diagnostic tests) **rendered by non-physician medical personnel are covered under Part B of the program** when they are furnished as incident to a physician's professional services. In order for such services to be covered under the "incident to" provision, the services must be furnished by an employee of the physician (or physician-directed clinic) and they must be services of kinds which are commonly furnished in physicians' offices. (It should be noted also, with respect to the social worker, that only those services that are medically relevant would fall within this provision.) In addition, the services must be performed under the immediate personal supervision of the physician, and the physician (or physician-directed clinic) must include in his or her bill the charge for his or her employee's services. In the case of a physician directed clinic, if the physician is on the clinic's premises while paramedical services are being performed and the physician is immediately available when needed, the direct supervision requirement may be considered to be met.

2. The **incident to** provision does not apply to services performed by a psychometrist employed and supervised by a qualified psychologist. Section 1861 (S) (2) (A) of the Medicare Law extends coverage to services performed by ancillary personnel where the services are rendered as incident to a physician's professional services. Since a psychologist is not considered a physician within the scope of the law, the "incident to" provision cannot apply and the services of ancillary personnel cannot be covered.

3. The services rendered by paramedical personnel which are claimed by a mental health center or physician directed clinic are **only allowable in the clinic (office) setting**, since immediate availability of a supervisory physician is required. Therefore, paramedic's services in home, nursing home, or hospital are not covered.

4. Part B of Medicare provides coverage for the diagnosis and treatment of mental, psycho-neurotic or personality disorders. Consult the American Psychiatric Association's **Diagnostic and Statistical Manual of Mental Disorders** for definition of terms. The limitation applies only to expenses incurred for physicians' services rendered in connection with one of these psychiatric conditions (with no distinction being made between the services of psychiatrists and non-psychiatric physicians), and any items or supplies furnished by the physician.

5. Counseling to family members to help them understand or accept the patient is **not covered.**

G. A psychiatric services limitation **applies** to expenses incurred for physicians' services.

1. **Regardless of the actual expenses** for physicians' services incurred in connection with the treatment of mental, psychoneurotic or personality disorders of persons who are not inpatients of hospitals, the amount of such expenses that can be counted in a calendar year is limited to the lesser of $312.50 or 62.5 percent of **the reasonable charges**. The computation of psychiatric expenses for deductible purposes is also subject to the 62.5 percent rule. Since $312.50 represents 62.5 percent of $500, any amount of non-inpatient psychiatric service expense incurred after the reasonable charge limit of $500 has been reached would not be covered and, therefore, would not be considered in computing incurred expense subject to reimbursement. Consequently, no reasonable charge determination is necessary on future billings during that calendar year for such treatment once the $500 reasonable charge limitation has been reached. Since the program's share of covered incurred expenses (after the $60 deductible) is 80 percent of the reasonable charges, the maximum possible payment for services would be 80 percent of $312.50, i.e., $250. This maximum could be reached only if the individual has had $60 of allowed charges other than non-inpatient psychiatric service expenses. Where the beneficiary does not have any incurred expenses other than the non-inpatient psychiatric service expenses, the maximum possible payment by the program would be $202.

2. Charges for **initial diagnostic services** (i.e., psychiatric testing and evaluation used to diagnose the patient's illness) **are not** subject to this limitation. The limitation is applied only to therapeutic services. Thus, three types of diagnostic services would be exempt from the limitation:

   (A) **Psychiatric testing**—this refers to the use of actual testing instruments such as intelligence tests.

   (B) **Psychiatric consultations**—evaluation made by a physician for the purpose of preparing a report for the attending physician.

   (C) **Initial psychiatric visits**—evaluation made by the physician who will treat the patient.

3. To compute the psychiatric **services limitation**:

   (A) Consider all psychiatric reasonable charges up to a maximum of $500, whether or not applied to the deductible.

   (B) Multiply by .625.

   (C) Subtract any unsatisfied deductible.

   (D) Multiply by .8.

4. The **limitation applies only** to expenses incurred for physicians' services rendered in connection with psychiatric conditions, and any items or supplies furnished by the physician in his own office.

5. Services furnished by other health personnel including home health services and outpatient hospital services would not be subject to the special psychiatric limitation even though the services are in connection with a condition included in the definition of **mental, psychoneurotic, and personality disorders.**

6. However, when the beneficiary receives non-covered physicians' services, the services, the services of auxiliary personnel who are rendering services **incident to** the physician's professional service also would not be covered. Therefore, once the yearly reasonable charge limitation of $500 for physicians' psychiatric services has been reached, there would be no program reimbursement for either the physician's services rendered **incident to** the physician's professional services when the services are for the treatment of a mental, psychoneurotic, or personality disorder.

7. Where the physician's services rendered are both for a psychiatric condition and one or more non-psychiatric conditions, **it will be necessary to separate the charges** for the psychiatric aspects of treatment from the charges for the non-psychiatric aspects of treatment. However, in any case in which the psychiatric and non-psychiatric components are not readily distinguishable, all of the charges will be allocated to the primary diagnosis.

V. Claim Form

A. **Completion of Medicare (SSA-1490) Claim Form** — Proper completion of this claim form reduces correspondence and speeds payment for services rendered. All items that apply to your claim are important, but the 6 items (claim plus bills) or 14 items (assignment case) marked on the sample claim form are essential. **Sample 57, page 185.**

B. **Part I — to be completed by patient.**

1. Please **print name** as indicated on Health Insurance claim card.

    The importance of the patient's name being completed correctly cannot be over-emphasized. "Mr." or "Mrs." is insignificant and need not be shown. Nicknames or abbreviated names also should be avoided. To ensure accuracy, the name should be taken from the patient's Medicare card, whether it is accurate or not. If the Medicare card is wrong, the patient should notify the District Social Security Administration Office and continue using the name on the card until a corrected card is issued.

2. The **Health Insurance Claim Number (HIC)** is equally as important as is the patient's name, and this information also should come from the Medicare card. The HIC is a nine digit number followed by an alphabetical suffix. The suffix may contain two alphabetical characters or an alphabetical character with another digit (i.e., 403-00-000 J1). A Medicare HIC number with an alphabetical prefix followed by six digits (i.e., MA 100201) indicates the patient is a railroad retiree, and the claim should be sent to Travelers Insurance Company. Some railroad retirees' HICs look exactly like the regular Medicare HIC and it is impossible to determine them from just looking at the numbers. The claim will be processed in the normal manner, except it will reject when the master beneficiary records, maintained by the Social Security Administration in Baltimore, are checked.

    Please check **male** or **female**, as there are some instances when it is impossible to determine the sex by the first name. The name, HIC, and sex must match the records maintained by the Social Security Administration or the claim will be delayed in processing until the error is resolved.

3. **Patient's address**—This block must be completed showing the patient's current mailing address, street number, city, state, and zip code. Failure to indicate the zip code will delay processing, as an address must have a zip code before payment can be made. If the provider is not accepting assignment, payment will be mailed directly to this address. If available, the patient's phone number may be of assistance.

4. **Description of the illness or injury** may be left blank, if item 7D, Part II, of the claim form is completed. Otherwise, complete this block.

   We need the physician's diagnosis. If not known, then provisional diagnosis complaints or symptoms are musts. We also need accident data for emergency first aid and the date of onset of symptoms is required for emergency medical care.

   The item relating to employment connected illness or injury should always be checked. Any injury or disease which look as if it may be employment related (i.e., black lung disease) must be investigated. If this item is not completed, the processing of the claim could be delayed.

5. If patient expects other health insurance or a welfare agency to **pay part of the expenses**, complete Item 5.

6. **Signature Requirements—Beneficiary**. The current Medicare requirements and alternatives for completion of the beneficiary's signature in Block 6 of the Medicare Request for Payment, SSA-1490 are as follows:

   (A) A Request for Payment **signed** by the beneficiary must be filed with each claim. The beneficiary's signature in Block 6 of the SSA-1490 not only authorizes release of necessary medical information to process the claim, but also permits the physician or supplier to accept assignment if the physician or supplier so wishes. (The beneficiary is not required to assign payment.)

   (B) If the beneficiary is unable to sign the Request for Payment, a representative, relative, friend, representative of an institution providing the Beneficiary care or support, or of a governmental agency providing him or her assistance (e.g., caseworker) **may sign for the beneficiary**. If someone other than the beneficiary has signed, then the signature block must include the beneficiary's name, the complete name and address of the person signing the claim, and the reason the beneficiary is unable to sign and the relationship to the beneficiary to the individual signing. (Only in very rare instances when the beneficiary is physically or mentally unable to sign and the beneficiary has no one else to sign on his or her behalf, may a physician, supplier, or clinic sign as a representative of the beneficiary. Such circumstances must be fully documented on the claim form.)

   (C) If services were rendered to a beneficiary prior to his or her death, but the beneficiary's signature was not obtained at the time of service, and the physician or supplier agrees to accept assignement, the word **Deceased** should be entered in Block 6 of the SSA-1490.

   (D) Generally, the beneficiary's authorization on the SSR-1490 **applies only to the particular service listed on the form**. However, if you are rendering services to a patient whose condition will require treatment over an extended period of time, regardless of whether you do or do not accept assignment, you may obtain the patient's signature on a one-time basis for the anticipated period of treatment. This authorization would cover any services rendered during that period for that particular illness or any other.

To properly submit claims under this provision, you must:

(1) Obtain the **patient's signature** in Block 6 of SSA-1490 (and date signed) and complete the SSA-1490 as you normally would do.

(2) The patient should **sign and date** a brief statement which would be attached to the above claim. The statement should be as follows:

"I request that payment under the medical insurance program be made either to me or to Dr._____on any bills for services furnished me by that physician during the period_____to _____."

This authorization would extend to the end of the period of treatment, but no later than the close of the calendar year. When the authorization is executed in the last three months of the year and the authorization would extend to no later than the close of the calendar year following.

(3) Subsequent claims submitted which are covered by this authorization would be noted in the signature area with **This treatment covered by previously obtained authorization for prolonged treatment.**

(4) Physicians or suppliers submitting claims under this procedure and sending bills to patients should advise them and incorporate on any bills sent to them **that this bill(s) should not be used for Medicare purposes since a claim(s) has been or will be submitted to Medicare on your behalf.**

(E) The use of "signature on file" may be utilized **only** for **Machine-prepared claims (Computer Generated Claims) that are prior approved by the Medicare B carrier.** Approval may be requested for **assigned as well as nonassigned claims**. If you are computer billing or anticipate doing so, please contact your local office for further details.

7. **Part II—Report of Services—to be completed by physician of supplier.**

At this point in completing the claim you may elect to complete Part II of the claim form or attach an itemization statement. An itemized statement must contain the same information as shown in Part II. Refer to section on itemized bills for assistance. If such a statement is attached, the physician must complete Block 12 (assuming the assignement accepted) and sign his or her name in Block 14. If you are completing the claim form for the patient but are not accepting assignment, you need not sign Block 14 if the name and provider code is shown in Block 8.

The following are instructions for completing Part II of the Medicare claim form: **Sample 57, page 185.**

(A) Indicate the **dates** of each service or phase of treatment.

(B) Indicate the **place** of service—be specific—identify the place as outlined on the lower portion of this form.

Note: Should any or all of the services be performed in a laboratory, nursing home, hospital or other outside facility, list the name and address in Item 13.

(C) Fully **describe** the surgical or medical procedures or other services and supplies furnished for each date given.

(D) Describe the **diagnosis**, symptoms, or injury.

(E) Show **itemization** for each service rendered.

(1) Indicate the full name and address of the physician or supplier and the office telephone number. We suggest that the physician's first name be shown rather than just an initial as it is often difficult to identify the correct Dr. Smith, Brown, or Jones who performed services. In clinic or group practice situations, the name(s) of each physician who rendered services must be identified in addition to the corporate name of the group /clinic.

(2) Indicate the **total charges** and **payments**, if any, for this claim.

(3) This section must be completed to show whether payment will be made to the patient or to the provider. (See the Assignment Agreement). If neither block is checked, the claim will be processed as non-assigned. If you do not wish to accept assignment, it would still be advisable to check the non-assigned block.

(4) Show the name and address of outside facilities performing services or the facility where the billing provider performed services.

(5) The SSA-1490 **must** be signed by the provider rendering the services being billed on assigned claims. The provider's degree and the date of signature should be completed.

The signature of the provider should be that of the provider identified in Item 8 on the SSA-1490. A hand-written signature is preferable. However, the provider can authorize a person on his or her staff (nurse, secretary, billing clerk, etc.) to sign the provider's name manually or by stamp in lieu of a hand written signature. The rubber-stamp signature may be a facsimile type of stamp that produces an impression identical or similar to the provider's signature.

Further clarification concerning signature requirements in special situations such as machine prepared billing, claims filed by a billing service or association, etc., should be directed to your local office.

VI. **Billing Statements**

A. Billing statements should clearly indicate **who the services are for**. It is preferable that the statements be prepared for each member of the family and the statement should include the diagnosis and HIC number.

B. When more than one service is performed, **indicate each service separately with a separate charge (itemization)**. Hand written statements should be legible with an adequate space between services. The same itemization is needed on a billing statement as on a claim form, since the same evaluations will be made on either one.

C. Whenever a balance due statement is sent to a Medicare beneficiary (deductible co-insurance, etc.,) and it is not intended for Medicare billing (lack of itemization, etc.,) please stamp or type, **BILL NOT FOR MEDICARE PURPOSES** on the face of the statement.

D. When there is **more than one provider** in an office, please indicate the name of the provider who performed the service. Indicate the name of the ordering/treating physician. Always include diagnosis, description of illness and/or injury.

E. On a continuous billing statement, please cross out charges previously filed with Medicare and write in **Medicare filed**. This type of statement is most difficult to process and almost always results in delay. This type of statement is not recommended for Medicare claim filing.

SAMPLE 55

MAJOR INSURANCE REIMBURSEMENT FORM

HEALTH INSURANCE
CLAIM FORM

READ INSTRUCTIONS BEFORE COMPLETING OR SIGNING THIS FORM

TYPE OR PRINT ☐ MEDICARE ☐ MEDICAID ☐ CHAMPUS ☐ OTHER

PATIENT & INSURED (SUBSCRIBER) INFORMATION

1 PATIENT'S NAME (First name, middle initial, last name)	2 PATIENT'S DATE OF BIRTH	3 INSURED'S NAME (First name, middle initial, last name)

4 PATIENT'S ADDRESS (Street, city, state, ZIP code)	5 PATIENT'S SEX MALE ☐ FEMALE	6 INSURED'S I.D. No. or MEDICARE No. (Include any letters)
	7 PATIENT'S RELATIONSHIP TO INSURED SELF SPOUSE CHILD OTHER	8 INSURED'S GROUP NO. (Or Group Name)

9 OTHER HEALTH INSURANCE COVERAGE - Enter Name of Policyholder and Plan Name and Address and Policy or Medical Assistance Number	10 WAS CONDITION RELATED TO: A PATIENT'S EMPLOYMENT YES ☐ NO B AN AUTO ACCIDENT YES ☐ NO	11 INSURED'S ADDRESS (Street, city, state, ZIP code)

12 PATIENT'S OR AUTHORIZED PERSON'S SIGNATURE (Read back before signing) I Authorize the Release of any Medical Information Necessary to Process this Claim and Request Payment of MEDICARE CHAMPUS Benefits Either to Myself or to the Party Who Accepts Assignment Below SIGNED DATE	13 I AUTHORIZE PAYMENT OF MEDICAL BENEFITS TO UNDERSIGNED PHYSICIAN OR SUPPLIER FOR SERVICE DESCRIBED BELOW SIGNED (Insured or Authorized Person)

PHYSICIAN OR SUPPLIER INFORMATION

14 DATE OF: ILLNESS (FIRST SYMPTOM) OR INJURY (ACCIDENT) OR PREGNANCY (LMP)	15 DATE FIRST CONSULTED YOU FOR THIS CONDITION	16 HAS PATIENT EVER HAD SAME OR SIMILAR SYMPTOMS? YES ☐ NO

17 DATE PATIENT ABLE TO RETURN TO WORK	18 DATES OF TOTAL DISABILITY FROM THROUGH	DATES OF PARTIAL DISABILITY FROM THROUGH

19 NAME OF REFERRING PHYSICIAN	20 FOR SERVICES RELATED TO HOSPITALIZATION GIVE HOSPITALIZATION DATES ADMITTED DISCHARGED

21 NAME & ADDRESS OF FACILITY WHERE SERVICES RENDERED (If other than home or office)	22 WAS LABORATORY WORK PERFORMED OUTSIDE YOUR OFFICE? YES ☐ NO CHARGES

23 DIAGNOSIS OR NATURE OF ILLNESS OR INJURY. RELATE DIAGNOSIS TO PROCEDURE IN COLUMN D BY REFERENCE TO NUMBERS 1, 2, 3, ETC. OR DX CODE ▼

1.
2.
3.
4.

24 A DATE OF SERVICE	B PLACE OF SERVICE	C PROCEDURE CODE (IDENTIFY)	FULLY DESCRIBE PROCEDURES, MEDICAL SERVICES OR SUPPLIES FURNISHED FOR EACH DATE GIVEN (EXPLAIN UNUSUAL SERVICES OR CIRCUMSTANCES)	D. DIAGNOSIS CODE	E CHARGES	F

25 SIGNATURE OF PHYSICIAN OR SUPPLIER (Read back before signing) SIGNED DATE	26 ACCEPT ASSIGNMENT (GOVERNMENT CLAIMS ONLY) (SEE BACK) YES ☐ NO 30 YOUR SOCIAL SECURITY NO.	27 TOTAL CHARGE	28 AMOUNT PAID	29 BALANCE DUE
		31 PHYSICIAN'S OR SUPPLIER'S NAME, ADDRESS, ZIP CODE & TELEPHONE NO.		

32 YOUR PATIENT'S ACCOUNT NO.	33 YOUR EMPLOYER I.D. NO.	
		I.D. NO.

● PLACE OF SERVICE CODES

1 — (IH) — INPATIENT HOSPITAL	4 — (H) — PATIENT'S HOME	7 — (NH) — NURSING HOME	O — (OL) — OTHER LOCATIONS
2 — (OH) — OUTPATIENT HOSPITAL	5 — DAY CARE FACILITY (PSY)	8 — (SNF) — SKILLED NURSING FACILITY	A — (IL) — INDEPENDENT LABORATORY
3 — (O) — DOCTOR'S OFFICE	6 — NIGHT CARE FACILITY (PSY)	9 — AMBULANCE	B — OTHER MEDICAL/SURGICAL FACILITY

APPROVED BY AMA COUNCIL ON MEDICAL SERVICE 8-74

SAMPLE 56

GOVERNMENT HEALTH INSURANCE FORM

MEDICAID REQUEST FOR PAYMENT

1. TX	2. Patient's Last Name	3. First Name	4. M.I.	5. Medicaid ID Number (Please check expiration date)

6. Patient's Address or Nursing Home visited - Number, Street, City, State & Zip Code

7. Patient's Date of Birth	8. If Patient was a referral, enter name of referring practitioner	9. Referring practitioner's Medicaid Provider Number
10. Prior Authorization Number, if applicable	11. Provider Patient Number, If applicable	

12.
Was patient involved in an accident? Yes ☐ No ☐

Was patient involved in on the job injury Yes ☐ No ☐

13. Does patient have Health Insurance other than Medicaid?

Yes ☐ No ☐

14. If Patient is eligible for Medicare or other insurance, file claim with Medicare or other insurance company first or indicate amount collected in Box 27 at bottom of form. State reason service will not be paid by Medicare or by other insurance company if no amount collected.

Company Name:

Policy Number:

15. (A) Primary Diagnosis	(A) Diagnosis Code
(B) Secondary Diagnosis	(B) Diagnosis Code

Indicate Diagnosis: (A) if Primary or both Primary and Secondary, and (B) if Secondary only; in Box 22 for each service

16. DATES OF SERVICE		17. PROCEDURE CODE	18. DESCRIPTION OF SERVICES If no Procedure Code in Box 17 fully describe Surgical or Medical Procedures and other Services or Supplies.	19. Number Visits/ Units of Service	20. If Family Planning Enter Y	21. Place of Service (1)	22. Diagnosis Treated Enter (A) or (B)	23. CHARGE
FROM Mo/Da/Yr	THRU Mo/Da/Yr							

24. Provider Name and Address

	25. TOTAL CHARGE	
26. Provider Number	27. Less Amount Received from Other Sources	

(1) PLACE OF SERVICE CODES: BOX 21
O-Doctor's Office   OH-Outpatient Hospital
IL-Independent Laboratory   SN-Skilled Nursing Home
H-Patient's Home   IC-Intermediate Care Facility
IH-Inpatient Hospital   OL-Other Location

28. Specialty Code	29. NET CHARGE
30. Telephone Number	31. Billing Date (Mo/Da/Yr)

Mail Completed Forms To:

32. Signature of Provider (Read reverse side prior to signature) "This is to certify that the foregoing information is true, accurate, and complete. I understand that payment and satisfaction of this claim will be from Federal and State funds, and that any false claims, statements, or documents, or concealment of a material fact, may be prosecuted under applicable Federal or State laws"

Signed:

EARLY PERIODIC SCREENING DIAGNOSIS AND TREATMENT (EPSDT)

33. Was an examination performed for the EPSDT program?

Yes ☐ No ☐

34. In the course of screening for the EPSDT program, indicate detection of:

1 - Visual Problems   3 - Hearing Problems
2 - Dental Problems   4 - Lead Poisoning
          5 - Other Problems

35. As a result of the screening, was further diagnosis and/or treatment required?

Yes ☐ No ☐

21E-001 R1

SAMPLE 57

GOVERNMENT HEALTH INSURANCE FORM

REQUEST FOR MEDICARE PAYMENT

MEDICAL INSURANCE BENEFITS—SOCIAL SECURITY ACT (See Instructions on Back—**Type or Print Information**)

Form Approved
OMB No
72-RO730

NOTICE—Anyone who misrepresents or falsifies essential information requested by this form may upon conviction be subject to fine and imprisonment under Federal Law

PART I—PATIENT TO FILL IN ITEMS 1 THROUGH 6 ONLY

When completed, send this form to:

Copy from **YOUR OWN HEALTH INSURANCE CARD** (See example on back)

1 Name of patient (First name, Middle initial, Last name)

2 Health insurance claim number (Include all letters) ☐ Male ☐ Female

3 Patient's mailing address · City, State, ZIP code · Telephone Number

4 Describe the illness or injury for which you received treatment (Always fill in this item if your doctor does not complete Part II below) · Was your illness or injury connected with your employment? ☐ Yes ☐ No

5 If you have other health insurance or if your State medical assistance agency will pay part of your medical expenses and you want information about this claim released to the insurance company or State agency upon its request, give the following information.

Insuring organization or State agency name and address · Policy or Medical Assistance Number

6 I authorize any holder of medical or other information about me to release to the Social Security Administration or its intermediaries or carriers any information needed for this or a related Medicare claim. I permit a copy of this authorization to be used in place of the original, and request payment of medical insurance benefits either to myself or to the party who accepts assignment below.

Signature of patient (See instructions on reverse where patient is unable to sign) · Date signed

SIGN HERE ▶

PART II—PHYSICIAN OR SUPPLIER TO FILL IN 7 THROUGH 14

7	A. Date of each service	B. Place of service (*See Codes below)	C. Fully describe surgical or medical procedures and other services or supplies furnished for each date given	D. Nature of illness or injury requiring services or supplies	E. Charges (If related to unusual circumstances explain in 7C)	Leave Blank
					$	

8 Name and address of physician or supplier (Number and street, city, State, ZIP code) · Telephone No. · **9** Total charges $ · **10** Amount paid $ · Physician or supplier code 1 2 3 7 0 · **11** Any unpaid balance due $

12 Assignment of patient's bill ▶ ☐ I accept assignment (See reverse) ☐ I do not accept assignment.

13 Show name and address of facility where services were performed (If other than home or office visits)

14 Signature of physician or supplier (A physician's signature certifies that physician's services were personally rendered by him or under his personal direction) · Date signed

*O—Doctor's Office
IL—Independent Laboratory
H—Patient's Home (If portable X-ray services, identify the supplier)
IH—Inpatient Hospital
ECF—Extended Care Facility
OH—Outpatient Hospital
OL—Other Locations
NH—Nursing Home

FORM SSA-1490 (8-72) · Department of Health, Education, and Welfare Social Security Administration

NOTES

SECTION XIII

FINANCIAL CONSIDERATIONS

NOTES

SECTION XIII

FINANCIAL CONSIDERATIONS

I. Financing the Practice

A. Initially, many individuals who consider opening a private practice **underestimate start-up costs**. They think in terms of renting office space, hanging out a shingle and commencing practice.

B. Upon a second glance, it becomes apparent there is a little more to it. The waiting room office and therapy rooms must be furnished. Lease, utility and telephone deposits must be made. File cabinets, business and therapy forms and supplies must be purchased. Insurance premiums must be paid in advance. Personnel must be hired. These can add up to a **staggering sum.**

C. During the first few months of private practice, you will likely encounter a **working capital crisis**. Accounts receivable will climb rapidly until you are able to bill and collect fees.

D. If you are starting on a full-time basis and have no other material sources of income, it will be necessary to provide for a **minimum amount of living expenses** until the practice can support you.

E. The summation of start-up costs, working capital requirements and living expenses equals the **total investment** that must be made. If you are like the majority of the populace, it will be necessary to borrow the major portion of this investment.

F. Life insurance policies and relatives are possible sources of borrowing. However, most individuals will choose to borrow from a lending institution. The lending institution will require a **Statement of Personal Financial Condition** so that it may evaluate your financial resources. **Sample 58, page 194** (commonly used format).

G. A **Projection of Cash Requirements** also should be presented to your lending institution. Be sure to document the figures with detailed lists and schedules. Your banker will be much more impressed if you provide, for example, a detailed equipment schedule listing exact descriptions, names of suppliers and exact costs, rather than "ball-parking" it, such as—Equipment, $5,000. **Sample 59, page 195.** (suggested format).

II. Accounting Methods

A. **Cash Basis Method**—Under this method, income is not recorded until the fees actually are collected. By the same token, expenses are not recorded until they actually are paid.

B. **Accrual Basis Method**—In contrast to the Cash Basis Method, income is recorded when earned and not when payment is received. Conceptually, the income has been earned the moment the therapy session ends. Expenses are recognized the moment they are incurred, regardless of when payment is made.

C. Most professional practices and service-type businesses utilize the **Cash Basis Method**. The reason is simple. Suppose that you started a practice and in that first year generated $50,000 of fees. But of that amount, $30,000 had been collected during the year and $20,000 still was due at the end of the year. Under the Cash

Basis Method, $30,000 of income would be reported on your tax return, but under the Accrual Basis Method, $50,000 would be reported. On the expense side of the ledger, the Accrual Basis Method, especially in your first year, normally will afford larger expense deductions than the Cash Basis Method. However, it seldom allows enough additional expense deductions to offset the increased income that would be reported.

III. Financial Statements

A. It is imperative that **periodic** (monthly, if possible) financial statements be prepared.

B. The **Balance Sheet** reflects the practice's financial position at a particular time. It displays all assets owned and all liabilities owed. The sample reflects accrual basis accounting; that is, accounts receivable and accounts payable have been reflected. **Sample 60, page 196.**

C. The **Statement of Earnings (Sample 61, page 197)** reflects cash-basis accounting; name of service rendered form-B sample 32. Form-B is then detached and stapled to paid. This method more nearly (but not exactly) matches what many people erroneously consider profits, i.e., cash left after paying the bills.

D. Several special purpose financial statements may be of some aid in certain circumstances. These include the **Statement of Changes in Financial Position, Statement of Sources and Uses of Cash, and Comparative Financial Statements.**

IV. Internal Controls

A. The busy professional is many time an easy target for those employees who are motivated to **misappropriate cash.**

B. The purpose of **proper internal controls** is to remove temptation and to divide responsibilities in such a way as to make misappropriation difficult without collusion.

C. On the following page is a checklist of procedures that will be of value in **reducing** the possiblity of employee theft. The checklist is intended only as a general guide and is not all encompassing.

INTERNAL CONTROLS CHECKLIST

A. **In General**

1. Prepare **periodic financial statements** to provide comparisons of income and expense accounts in order to spot significant fluctuations.

2. Secure **all** accounting documents during non-business hours.

3. The utilization of an **outside accountant** to review operations and procedures can sometimes bring irregular practices to light.

B. **Cash**

1. It possible, vest the **cash handling function** with a person other than the one posting transactions to the patient accounts.

2. In a small office with one clerical employee, the best procedure is for the professional to **pick up the mail** (through the use of a post office box), **make a list of the checks, and make the bank deposit**. The list can be given to the clerical employee for posting to the patient's accounts.

3. Sequentially **numbered cash receipts** should be used for all cash transactions.

4. Reconcile the bank statements **monthly**. If an employee prepares these checks, examine endorsements.

5. If a clerical employee prepares the checks for your signature, have him or her **present the invoice** with the checks.

C. Accounts Receivable

1. **Serially numbered** patient charge tickets should be used.

2. Patient **ledger cards** should be totaled and reconciled with the control account periodically.

3. All adjustments and write-offs should be **approved in writing** in advance by you.

4. A **separate control account** should be maintained for bad debts.

5. You should periodically **sample** the procedures by tracing a sample of cash receipts from the original cash records to the patient ledger cards.

6. **ABOVE ALL—BE VIGILANT—OBSERVE—ASK QUESTIONS**

V. Analysis of Accounts Receivable

A. **Accounts receivable** soon will become the largest (by far) financial asset the private practitioner possesses.

B. Proper management of accounts receivable is the **key to financial success.** Poor management is the quickest way to **financial ruin.**

C. A key measurement of management efficiency is the **Number of Days of Business Outstanding in Accounts Receivable. Sample 62, page 198.**

D. Further analysis, by payer, should be made. A **comparison of accounts receivable** by payer with total billings by payer can be revealing. For example, if it were discovered that 10% of the practice's billings were to the Full Coverage Insurance Company, but 20% of the accounts receivable were due from them, it might be concluded that a problem exists.

E. The **collection percentage** is also a valuable indicator. **Sample 63, page 199.**

VI. How to Increase Your Chances of Protecting Independent Contractor Status of Your Workers

A. The use of **independent contractors** as an ongoing component of your work force causes you to run the risk of having these people classified as employees rather than independent contractors. Such a reclassification would subject you to federal and state payroll taxes.

B. Regulations, ruling, and court cases have established **twenty common law factors** for determination of the worker's status. **Samples 64-65, pages 200-206.**

C. In order to increase your chances of classifying a worker as an **independent contractor:**

1. You should not require the workers to work a minimum number of hours per day or week.

2. The worker should pay his own expenses, such as licenses, liability and health insurance, transportation expenses, etc.

3. Workers should not be provided with office space, nor should they be allowed to use your equipment.

4. Workers should not be required to work for you exclusively. They must be allowed to provide their services to others.

5. Generally, payment by the job should be made rather than by the hour or week.

6. You should not provide them with training, uniforms or other items that identify them with your firm.

7. No fringe benefits, such as vacation pay, sick pay, bonuses, or group insurance should be provided.

8. In essence, it is not enough that the worker appears to be an independent contractor; he or she must in reality be one.

VII. Selection of Business Consultants

A. Depending on the size, scope, and nature of your practice you will need the counsel of **various types of consultants.**

B. At a **minimum**, you will need a banker, attorney, accountant, and insurance broker. As the **practice grows** in size and complexity, it may be necessary to deal with pension engineers, personnel consultants, trust fund administrators and industrial engineers.

C. In selecting these people, seek those that have **some exposure to your type of business**. Many attorney's, for example, specialize in non-business areas (torts, injuries, divorces) and you would probably be more comfortable with an attorney who does business-related work.

D. **Utilize one consultant to find the others**. If you have found an attorney you like, ask him or her for the names of accountants he or she respects. Usually, he or she will give you a list of three or four competent ones and let you make a selection. Most business professionals will not give just one name, as they feel they should not exert undue influence on your selection.

E. **Interview your candidates**. Ask about their experience and backgrounds. Find out if they handle other clients similar to you (they are bound by ethics not to reveal the name of their clients, but they can give you an idea of the kind of clients they handle).

F. As an example, re-read the section on incorporating and taxation before talking to prospective accountants. Ask them questions on that section and **attempt to ascertain their knowledge.**

G. **Do not be impressed by the trappings**. Just because they have a large, expensively furnished office, do not automatically choose them. The large firm may not be interested in your small account or they may not have the time to service you properly. Sometimes, the enthusiastic, young business professional is just what you need.

H. **Do not accept their advice blanketly**. Make them explain it in your language. Do not be silent just because you do not understand what they are saying. . .remember, they do not understand you when you start talking about biofeedback, thermal trainers, diagnostic labels, and the DSM III.

I. **Use their time wisely**. They, like you, are expensive, so use them on the big or difficult things and do the little things yourself.

SAMPLE 58

JOHN DOE, PH. D.
STATEMENT OF PERSONAL FINANCIAL CONDITION
December 31, 19XX

ASSETS

Cash in Checking (1st Nat's Bank—#123-4567-8)	$ 800	
Cash in Savings (City Savings Bank—#444-2372-0)	6,550	$ 7,350
Cash Value Life Insurance (Mutual Life Policy #914738)		2,850
Note Receivable (R.J. Jones—Due 6/30/85)		1,000
400 Shares Common—ABC Corporation @ $20 Market		8,000
Personal Residence (111 Main St.) @ Market	$50,000	
Rental Property (112 Main St.) @ Market	30,000	80,000
Automobile (1982 Zipmobile) @ Market	7,500	
Automobile (1980 Zipmobile) @ Market	2,000	
Household Goods @ Market	8,000	
Coin Collection @ Market	2,000	19,500
		$ 118,700

LIABILITIES

Department Store Charges and Credit Cards	$ 1,500	
Federal and State Income Taxes Due	750	
Automobile Loan Due (1st Nat'l Bank—$175 mo. payment)	5,500	
Mortgage Payable (Residence—1st Nat'l Bank—$390 mo. payment)	39,200	
Mortgage Payable (Rental-City Savings-$180 mo. payment)	15,600	
		$ 62,550

EXCESS ASSETS OVER LIABILITIES $ 56,150

CURRENT INCOME SOURCES

Salary—State University	$27,000
Rental Income	3,000
Interest and Dividends	1,000
	$31,000

SAMPLE 59

PROJECTION OF CASH REQUIREMENTS

Pre-Opening Expenses

Equipment	$ xx,xxx		
Supplies	x,xxx		
Utility/Telephone Deposits	x,xxx		
Lease Deposits	x,xxx		
Advertising/Announcements	x,xxx		
Licenses/Permits	x,xxx		
Insurance Pre-payments	x,xxx		
	$ xx,xxx		

	1st Month	2nd Month	3rd Month
Fees	$ xx,xxx	$ xx,xxx	$ xx,xxx
	$ xx,xxx	$ xx,xxx	$ xx,xxx
Direct Costs	xx,xxx	xx,xxx	xx,xxx
Administration and Overhead	xx,xxx	xx,xxx	xx,xxx
Loan Payments	xx,xxx	xx,xxx	xx,xxx
Personal Living Expenses	$ xx,xxx	$ xx,xxx	$ xx,xxx
CASH FLOW—POSITIVE (NEGATIVE)	$ xx,xxx	$ xx,xxx	$ xx,xxx

1. See Sample 68 for detailed examples of the broad categories used above.
2. Be prepared to explain which expenses can be cut if fees do not meet expectations.
3. The projection should be extended for as many months as necessary until a positive cash flow is achieved. The summation of the negative cash flows to that point plus the pre-opening expenses is your cash requirement.

SAMPLE 60

PSYCHOLOGISTS ASSOCIATES
BALANCE SHEET
December 31, 19XX

ASSETS

Current Assets:

Petty Cash		$ xxx	
Cash in Bank-Operating Account		x,xxx	
Cash in Bank-Tax Account		x,xxx	
Accounts Receivable-Patients	$ xxx,xxx		
Less Allowance for Uncollectible	xx,xxx	xxx,xxx	
Employee Advances		xxx	
			$ xxx,xxx

Property and Equipment:

Furniture and Fixtures	$ xx,xxx		
Accumulated Depreciation	x,xxx	$ xx,xxx	
Leasehold Improvement	$ xx,xxx		
Accumulated Depreciation	x,xxx	xx,xxx	
TOTAL ASSETS			$ xxx,xxx

LIABILITIES AND CAPITAL

Current Liabilities:

Notes Payable	$ xx,xxx	
Employee Payroll Taxes Withheld	x,xxx	
Employer Payroll Taxes Accrued	x,xxx	
Accounts Payable	x,xxx	
		$ xx,xxx

Capital:

Capital at Jan. 1	$ xx,xxx		
Add: Net Income Retained	x,xxx	$ xx,xxx	
Accrual-Basis Adjustments:			
Net Accounts Receivable	$ xxx,xxx		
Less Accounts Payable and Payroll Taxes Accrued	xx,xxx	xxx,xxx	
			$ xxx,xxx
TOTAL LIABILITIES AND CAPITAL			$ xxx,xxx

SAMPLE 61

PSYCHOLOGISTS ASSOCIATES
STATEMENT OF EARNINGS ON A CASH BASIS
FOR THE YEAR ENDED DECEMBER 31, 19XX

INCOME	THIS MONTH	PERCENT	YEAR TO DATE	PERCENT
Fees-Individual Therapy	$ x,xxx	xx.x%	$ x,xxx	xx.x%
Fees-Hypnotherapy	x,xxx	xx.x	x,xxx	xx.x
Fees-Marital Therapy	x,xxx	xx.x	x,xxx	xx.x
Fees-Group Therapy	x,xxx	xx.x	x,xxx	xx.x
TOTAL FEES	$ xx,xxx	100.0%	$ xx,xxx	100.0%
DIRECT COST				
Professional Staff Salaries	x,xxx	xx.x%	x,xxx	xx.x%
Consultants Fees	x,xxx	xx.x	x,xxx	xx.x
Therapy Supplies	x,xxx	xx.x	x,xxx	xx.x
Professional Equipment Rental	x,xxx	xx.x	x,xxx	xx.x
Professional Staff-Payroll				
Taxes and Fringes	x,xxx	xx.x	x,xxx	xx.x
Depreciation-Prof. Equip.	x,xxx	xx.x	x,xxx	xx.x
	$ xx,xxx	xx.x%	$ xx,xxx	xx.x%
ADMINISTRATION AND OVERHEAD				
Advertising	x,xxx	xx.x	x,xxx	xx.x
Collection Expense	x,xxx	xx.x	x,xxx	xx.x
Depreciation	x,xxx	xx.x	x,xxx	xx.x
Dues and Subscriptions	x,xxx	xx.x	x,xxx	xx.x
Office Equipment Rental	x,xxx	xx.x	x,xxx	xx.x
Interest	x,xxx	xx.x	x,xxx	xx.x
Insurance	x,xxx	xx.x	x,xxx	xx.x
Legal and Accounting	x,xxx	xx.x	x,xxx	xx.x
Maintenance & Repair	x,xxx	xx.x	x,xxx	xx.x
Office Supplies	x,xxx	xx.x	x,xxx	xx.x
Office Salaries	x,xxx	xx.x	x,xxx	xx.x
Office Staff-Payroll				
Taxes & Fringes	x,xxx	xx.x	x,xxx	xx.x
Postage	x,xxx	xx.x	x,xxx	xx.x
Rent	x,xxx	xx.x	x,xxx	xx.x
Telephone	x,xxx	xx.x	x,xxx	xx.x
Utilities	x,xxx	xx.x	xx.x	xx.x
	$ xx,xxx	xx.x%	$ xx,xxx	xx.x
Net Earnings	$ x,xxx	xx.x%	$ x,xxx	xx.x%
Funds Withdrawn	x,xxx	xx.x	x,xxx	xx.x
Earnings Retained in Business	$ x,xxx	xx.x%	$ x,xxx	xx.x%

SAMPLE 62

CALCULATION OF THE NUMBER OF DAYS OF

Month	Gross Charges	Discounts	Net Charges	Bad Debts	Collections
Jan	$ 13,250	$ 175	$ 13,075	$ 500	$ 10,400
Feb	15,100	275	14,825	-0-	13,750
Mar	12,975	450	12,525	1,200	13,225
Apr	17,200	600	16,600	950	17,900
May	11,400	150	11,250	1,750	10,400
Jun	12,825	325	12,500	350	16,100
6 mos. total	$ 82,750	$1,975	$ 80,775	$4,750	$81,775

To determine the accounts receivable balance at the end of the month, add the accounts receivable balance at the beginning of the month to the gross charges for the month. From that figure deduct discounts, bad debts, and collections. For example, if our January 1 accounts receivable balance was $100,000, the above formula would tell us that the balance at January 31 would be $102,175. The June 30 accounts receivable balance would be $94,250.

To calculate the number of days of business outstanding, first determine an applicable time frame. In the example, a 181 day period from January 1 to June 30 was used.

A. **The number of business days in the period**: Assume you are open every day of the week except a half-day on Saturday and all day on Sunday. Count the number of days in the time frame (counting Saturdays as half-days). Assume that equals 143.

B. Next, it is necessary to ascertain the **average per-business day charges**. For this calculation ignore discounts since they normally are determined at the time of service and therefore become immediately uncollectable. Divide net charges by the number of business days. The sample company is generating $564.86 per business day in charges ($80,775 ÷ 143).

C. Divide the ending accounts receivable balance (June 30 balance was $94,250) by the net charges per business day ($564.86) and discover that the firm has 166.9 **days of business out-standing.**

What does this number (166.9) indicate? It is a measurement of efficiency in collecting accounts. The sample company has worked 5½ months for which it has not been paid. This is not an enviable record, and it indicates a **problem in the collection procedure.**

By charting this index through time, collection efficiency can be measured by a constant. Fluctuating charges or collections do not affect the validity of the statistic. By calculating the February 1 to July 31 measurement and comparing it to the January 1 to June 30 measurement, one can check the **progress of the collection effort.**

SAMPLE 63

CALCULATION OF COLLECTION PERCENTAGES

The calculation of collection percentages is an important measurement of collection effort. The ideal, of course, is **100%.**

The computation of this is quite simple, and for our example assume the same charges and collections as displayed on **Sample 74, page 214.**

Merely divide the collections for the period by the net charges. Now we come to the tricky part. If you divide June collections by June charges, has a valid statistic been derived? No, because most of the June collections will probably be May, April, and other months charges.

Assume that an analysis indicates that most of the collections are for accounts charged in the March 1 to June 30 period. (Calculation of the number of business days outstanding in accounts receivable as explained in **Sample 74** would be a good indicator of the time frame). If the March 1 to June 30 period is the correct period, then net charges for the period should be averaged before calculating the collection percentage. The example indicates average monthly charges for the March 1 to June 30 period to be $13,219. The collection percentage for June therefore is $16,000 collections by $13,219 or 121.8%. (June was steady, but May was only 75.4%.)

SAMPLE 64

EMPLOYEE VS. INDEPENDENT CONTRACTOR

Due to the ever-increasing Social Security and Unemployment tax rate, many employers now are attempting to avoid these taxes by declaring that their **employees are independent contractors**. There is no easy determination of this status, but the following checklist should aid in making a determination.

For FICA, FUTA and income tax withholding purposes, the term **employee** (Secs. 3121(d), 3306(i) and 3401(c) includes any individual who, under the usual common law rules applicable in determining the employer-employee relationship, has the status of an employee.

THE COMMON LAW RULES—FACTORS:

Under the common law test, a worker is an employee if the employer for whom he or she is working has the RIGHT to direct and control that person in the manner he or she works, both as to the final results and as to the details of when, where, and how the work is to be completed. THE EMPLOYER NEED NOT ACTUALLY EXERCISE CONTROL; IT IS SUFFICIENT THAT HE HAS THE RIGHT TO DO SO.

If the relationship of employer and employee exists, it is of no consequence whether the employee is designated as a partner, co-adventurer, agent or independent contractor. Furthermore, all classes or grades or employees are included within the relationship of employer and employee. Thus, superintendents, manager, and other supervisory personnel are employees.

The factors or elements which indicate control are outlined below in a list of 20 items. Any single item or small group of items is not conclusive evidence concerning the presence or absence of control.

These common law factors are now always found in every case. Some do not apply to certain occupations. The consideration to be given each factor is not always equal. The degree of importance of each factor may vary depending upon the occupation and the reason for its existence. Therefore, in each case we will have two things to weigh: first, does the factor exist; and second, what is the reason for or importance of its existence or non-existence?

1. **INSTRUCTIONS.** A person who must comply with instructions about when, where, and how he or she must work is usually an employee. Some employees can work without receiving directives because they are highly skilled and conscientious workers. However, the control element is present if the employer has the option of requiring compliance with the directives. The directives which show how to reach the desired result may be spoken or written (manuals or procedures).

2. **TRAINING.** Training someone by having an experienced employee work with that person by correspondence, by required attendance at meetings, or by other methods indicates that the employer wants the services performed in a set method or manner. This is especially true if the training is given periodically or at frequent intervals. An INDEPENDENT CONTRACTOR ordinarily uses his own methods and receives no training from the purchaser of his services. In fact, it is usually his methodology which brings him or her to the attention of the purchaser.

3. **INTEGRATION**. Integration of the person's services into the business operations generally shows that the individual is subject to direction and control. In applying the integration test, first determine the scope and function of the business and then whether the services of the individual are merged into it. When the success or continuation of a business depends to an appreciable degree upon the performance of certain services, the persons who perform those services must necessarily be subject to a certain amount of control by the owner of the business.

4. **SERVICES RENDERED PERSONALLY**. If the services must be performed personally, presumably the employer is interested in the methods, as well as the results. He is interested in not only the result, but also the worker.

5. **HIRING, SUPERVISING, AND PAYING ASSISTANTS**. Hiring, overseeing, and paying assistants by the employer generally shows control over the people on the job. Sometimes one worker may hire, supervise, and pay the other workers. He or she may do so as a result of a contract under which he or she agrees to provide materials and labor and under which he or she is responsible for only the attainment of a result. In this case, he or she is an independent contractor. Nevertheless, if he or she hires, supervises, and pays workers at the direction of the employer, he or she may be an employee acting in the capacity of a foreman for or representative of the employer. (Rev. Rul. 70-440, IRB 1970-34, 16).

6. **CONTINUING RELATIONSHIP**. A continuing relationship between a worker and the person for whom he or she performs services is a factor which indicates that an employer-employee relationship exists. Continuing services may include work performed at frequently recurring, though somewhat irregular, intervals either on call of the employer or whenever the work is available. If the arrangement contemplates continuing or recurring work, the relationship is considered permanent even if the services are part-time, seasonal, or of short duration.

7. **SET HOURS OF WORK**. The institution of set hours of work by the employer is a factor indicating control. This condition bars the worker from being master of his or her own time, which is the right of the independent contractor. If the nature of the occupation makes fixed hours impractical, a requirement that the worker work at certain times is an element of control.

8. **FULL-TIME REQUIRED**. If a person must devote complete time to the business of the employer, the employer has control over the amount of time the worker spends working and impliedly restricts him or her from doing other gainful work. An independent contractor, on the other hand, is free to work when and for whom he or she chooses. Full-time does not necessarily mean an eight hour day or a five or six day week. Its meaning may vary with the intent of the parties, the nature of the occupation, and the customs of a locality. These conditions should be considered when defining "full time."

Full-time services may be required even though not specified in writing or orally. For example, to produce a required minimum volume of business may compel a person to devote all working time to that business; or he or she may not be permitted to work for anyone else, and perhaps it is that to earn a living he or she necessarily must work full-time.

9. **DOING WORK ON EMPLOYER'S PREMISES**. Doing the work on the employer's premises in itself does not indicate control. However, it does imply that the employer has control, especially when the work is the kind that could be done elsewhere. A person working at the employer's place of business is physically within the employer's direction and supervision. The use of desk space and telephone and stenographic ser-

vices provided by the employer places the worker within the employer's direction and supervision. Work done off the premises indicates some freedom from control. However, this fact by itself does not mean that the worker is not an employee. Control over the place of work is indicated when the employer has the right to compel a person to travel a designated route, to canvass a territory within a certain time, or to work at specific places. In some occupations, services must be performed away from the premises of the employer; for example, employees of construction contractors or taxicab drivers.

10. **ORDER OR SEQUENCE SET**. If a worker must perform services in the sequence or established order set for him or her by the employer, it shows that the worker is not free to follow a self pattern of work, but must follow the established routines and schedules of the employer. Often, because of the nature of an occupation, the employer either does not set the order of the services or sets them infrequently. It is sufficient to show control, however, if he retains the right to do so. The outside commission salesman, for example, usually is permitted latitude in mapping out his activities and may work independently to a considerable degree. In many cases, however, at the direction of the employer, he must report to the office at specified times, follow up leads, and perform certain tasks at certain times. Such directions interfere with and take preference over the salesman's own routines or plans; this fact indicates control.

11. **ORAL OR WRITTEN REPORTS**. Another form of control is the request to submit regular oral or written reports to the employer. This action shows that the person is compelled to account for his or her actions. Such reports are useful to the employer for present controls or future supervision; that is, they enable him or her to determine whether instructions are being followed or, if the person has been working independently, whether new instructions should be issued.

12. **PAYMENT BY HOUR, WEEK, MONTH**. Payment by the hour, week, or month generally points to an employer-employee relationship, provided that this method of payment is not just a convenient way of paying a lump sum agreed upon as the cost of doing a job. The payment by a firm of regular amounts of stated intervals to a worker strongly indicates an employer-employee relationship. (The fact that payments are received from a third party, e.g., tips or fees, is irrelevant in determining whether an employment relationship exists).

The firm assumes that the hazard of the services of the worker will be proportionate to the regular payments. This action warrants the assumption that, to protect its investment, the firm has the right to direct and control the performance of the worker. It also is assumed in absence of evidence to the contrary that the worker, by accepting payment upon such a basis, has agreed that the firm shall have such right of control. Obviously, the firm expects the worker to give a day's work for a day's pay. Generally, a person is an employee if he is guaranteed a minimum salary or is given a drawing account of a specified amount at stated intervals and is not required to repay any excess drawn over commissions earned.

Payment made by the job or on a set commission often indicates that the person is an independent contractor. Payment by the job includes a lump sum computed by the number of hours required to do the job at a fixed rate per hour. Such a payment should not be confused with payment by the hour.

13. **PAYMENT OF BUSINESS AND/OR TRAVELING EXPENSES**. If the employer pays the person's business and/or traveling expenses, the person is ordinarily an employee. The employer, to be able to control expenses, must retain the right to regulate and direct the person's business activities.

Conversely, someone who is paid on a job basis, but now has to take care of all incidental expenses is generally an independent contractor. Since this person is only accountable personally for his or her expenses, that person is free to work according to his or her own methods and means.

14. **FURNISHING TOOLS, MATERIALS**: The fact that an employer supplies tools and materials tends to show the existence of an employer-employee relationship. Such an employer can determine which tools the person is to use and, to some extent, in what order and how they shall be used.

An independent contractor usually furnishes his or her own tools. Nevertheless, in some occupational fields, such as skilled workmen, workers customarily furnish their own tools. They are usually small hand tools. Such a practice does not necessarily indicate a lack of control over the services of the worker.

15. **SIGNIFICANT INVESTMENT**: Investment by an individual in facilities which he or she uses in performing services for another is a factor which tends to establish an independent contractor status. On the other hand, lack of investment indicates dependence on the employer for such facilities and, accordingly, the existence of an employer-employee relationship.

In general, facilities include equipment or premises necessary for the work, such as office furniture and machinery. This term does not include tools, instruments, or clothing, commonly provided by employees in their trade nor does it include education, experience, or training.

In order for an investment to be thought of as a significant factor in establishing that an employer-employee relationship does not exist, it must be REAL, it must be ESSENTIAL, and it must be ADEQUATE.

16. **REALIZATION OF PROFIT OR LOSS**: The person who can realize a profit or suffer a loss as a result of his or her services is generally an independent contractor, but the individual who cannot is an employee.

"Profit or loss" implies the use of capital by the individual in an independent business of his or her own. Thus, opportunity for higher earnings, such as from pay on a piecework basis or the possibility of gain or loss from a commission arrangement, is not considered profit or loss.

Whether a profit is realized or a loss suffered generally depends upon management decisions; that is, the one responsible for a profit or loss can use his or her own ingenuity, initiative, and judgement in conducting his business or enterprise. Opportunity for profit or loss may be established by one or more of a variety of circumstances, including the following examples:

1. The individual hires, directs, and pays assistants.

2. He or she has his or her own office, equipment, materials, or other work facilities.

3. The person has continuing and recurring liabilities or obligations, and his or her success or failure depends upon the relation of receipts to expenditures.

4. The person agrees to perform specific jobs for prices agreed upon in advance and to pay expenses incurred in connection with the work.

5. The person's services and/or those of his or her assistants establishes or affects his or her business reputation and not the reputation of those who purchase the services.

17. **WORKING FOR MORE THAN ONE FIRM AT A TIME**: A person who works for several persons or firms simultaneously is usually an independent contractor because he or she is free from control by any single firm. It is possible, however, for one person to work for several people or firms and still be an employee of one or all of them .

18. **MAKING SERVICE AVAILABLE TO GENERAL PUBLIC**: The fact that someone makes services available to the general public usually indicates an independent contractor relationship. An individual may offer services to the public in a number of ways: by having his or her own office and assistants; by hanging out a "shingle" in front of a home or office; by holding business licenses; by being listed in business directories or by maintaining business listings in telephone directories; or by advertising in newspapers, trade journals, or magazines.

19. **RIGHT TO DISCHARGE**: The right to dismiss is a major factor in indicating that the person possessing the right is an employer. The person exercises control through ever-present threat of dismissal, which causes the worker to obey his instructions. An independent contractor, on the other hand, cannot be fired so long as he or she produces a result which meets the contract specifications.

20. **RIGHT TO TERMINATE**: An employee has the right to conclude a relationship with an employer at anytime without incurring liability. An independent contractor usually agrees to complete a specific job; he or she is responsible for its satisfactory completion or legally obligated to make good for failure to complete the job.

We now have covered the 20 FACTORS under COMMON LAW FACTORS. We now will consider the second point: What is the reason for or importance of its existence or non-existence?

All facts must be weighed, and the decision must be based on cautious evaluations of these facts, IRS published rulings, and the presence or absence of factors which point to an employer-employee relationship or to an independent contractor status.

Take, for example, a beauty parlor. The shop owner may say that he or she does not control the hours, fix the amount charged for a haircut, or control the beautician's cleanliness. However, in determining the weight of each of these factors, we should consider the reason for their nonexistence. We might find that the union, in effect, controls the hours and sets the prices for haircuts and that the State Beauty Operators Board of Examiners controls the cleanliness of the parlor. We correctly conclude, then, that the weight to be given each of these factors is nothing.

In the case of a salesman, it might be found that the employer does not control the hours of work because to make a sale he or she may have to arrange hours to fit the customers' hours, such as calling in the evening when a husband and wife are home. This may be true of other occupations. The important thing is to weight any factor being considered according to its reason for existence or nonexistence.

FICA STATUTORY EMPLOYEE RULES:

In addition to common law employees, the FICA provides for statutory employees, which include the following:
   1. Agent drivers and commission drivers;
   2. Full-time life insurance salesmen;
   3. Home workers; and
   4. Traveling or city salesmen.

With regard to the statutory employee, the employer is required to withhold FICA only and report it along with that of his common law employees.

SAMPLE 65

EMPLOYMENT QUESTIONNAIRE

Firm
Name _____

Worker's
Name _____

Street _____

S.S. # _____

City _____State_____Dates Worked _____

Type _____Individual _____Partnership _____Corporation

_____Other (Explain in comments)

Principal business activity _____

Worker's occupation or title and description of his work.
(Explain in comments).

Why is the worker considered to be self-employed? (Answer in comments).

Answer the following questions—**YES, NO,** or **OTHER**. (If **OTHER**, explain in comments.)

1. Do you believe the firm has the RIGHT to supervise and control its workers? _____

2. Should a worker comply with instructions about when, where and how he or she should work? _____

3. Does the worker receive any training from the firm? _____

4. Are the worker's services worked into the business operations? _____

5. Does the worker render his services personally? _____

6. May the worker hire, supervise, and pay assistants at direction of firm? _____

7. Is there an on-going relationship between the worker and the firm? _____

8. Must the worker follow set hours of work? _____

9. Must the worker devote his full time to the business of the firm? _____

10. Must the work be done on the firm's premises? _____

11. Is the worker required to perform services in a set sequence established by the firm? _____

12. Are verbal or written reports required of the worker? _____

13. Are payments made periodically (hour-week-month)? _____

14. Is the worker guaranteed a minimum salary or payment? _____

15. Are the worker's business and/or traveling expenses paid by the firm?   _____

16. Does the firm furnish books and materials?   _____

17. Does the worker have a sizable investment in the firm?   _____

18. Is this investment real? essential? adequate?   _____

19. Can the worker realize a profit (loss) as a result of his services?   _____

20. May the worker do services for other firms at the same time?   _____

21. Are the worker's services available to the general public?   _____

22. Does the firm have the option of discharging the worker?   _____

23. May the worker terminate his relationship with the firm when he elects to do so?   _____

COMMENTS: (Identify by item, use extra pages, if necessary)

_____

_____

_____

_____

_____

SECTION XIV

TAX CONSIDERATIONS

NOTES

SECTION XIV

TAX CONSIDERATIONS

I. Advantages of Incorporating

A. Liability for some losses can be limited to the assets of the corporation; however, **malpractice is not one of them**. Even with the corporate form of organization, malpractice losses are personal in nature.

B. The federal (and state) income taxes **may be lower**. The federal income tax is currently 15% of the first $25,000 of taxable income, 18% of the next $25,000, 30% of the next $25,000, 40% of the next $25,000, and 46% of everything over $100,000.

C. Certain fringe benefits may be provided to the owners with **before-tax dollars** that cannot be provided with the non-corporate form of ownership. Examples include a qualified pension plan, group health insurance, disability insurance, life insurance, and medical expenses.

D. A corporation may elect to end its tax year on the last day of any month it chooses. The non-corporate form, with rare exceptions, must close its books on December 31 each year. This provision can be of **great help in tax planning.**

E. The shareholders may elect Sub-Chapter S Status. This election, under most circumstances, eliminates the federal income tax on the corporation. The income **passes through** and is taxed to the shareholders.

II. Disadvantages of Incorporating

A. Several transactions that normally are of no concern to the I.R.S. with the **partnership form** of organization are subject to its scrutiny with the **corporate form**, including the payment of salaries and withdrawals of funds.

B. The requirements of formality are stricter. This normally causes **higher fees** and **administrations costs** from attorneys, accountants, and pension consultants.

C. **Dividends are doubly taxed**: the corporation, at present, is not permitted to deduct the payment of dividends, so the recipient (subject to a $200 dividend exclusion) must report it as income. By contrast, the payment of a salary is deductible by the corporation and, of course, is taxable to the recipient.

D. The owner/operator, by virtue of causing the corporation to pay him a salary, subjects himself to **state and federal unemployment taxes** and **workman's compensation insurance**. The partner/proprietor is not subject to these laws.

E. The salary is subject to the **social security tax.** (In 1986, the owner/operator/employee pays 7.15% and the corporation pays another 7.15% of the first $42,000 of salary; by contrast, the partner/proprietor pays 12.3% of the first $42,000 of earnings.)

COMPARISON—VARIOUS ENTITY TYPES

	PROPRIETORSHIP	PARTNERSHIP	"REGULAR" CORPORATION	"SUB-CHAPTER S" CORPORATION
Limited Liability—Malpractice	No	No	No	No
Limited Liability—Other	No	No, except "Limited Partnerships"	In most cases	In most cases
Continuity of Business	No	Sometimes	Yes	Yes
Tax-Paying Entity	No	No	Yes	Usually not
Highest Possible Tax Rate	50%	50%	46%	50%
Are Distributions Taxable	No	Seldom	Usually	Depends on timing and nature of distribution
Can Owner Receive A Salary (In Normal Sense)	No	No	Yes	Yes
Is Owner Subject To Social Security Tax	Yes 12.3% of net earnings to a maximum of $42,000		Yes—if salary paid, then 7.15% of first $42,000 on employee, 7.15% of first $42,000 on corporation	
Is Unemployment Tax Deductible	N/A	N/A	Yes	Yes
Is Social Security Tax Deductible	No	No	Corporate share only	

COMPARISON-VARIOUS ENTITY TYPES

	PROPRIETORSHIP	PARTNERSHIP	"REGULAR" CORPORATION	"SUB-CHAPTER S" CORPORATION
Can Insurance on Owner's Life Be Set Up To Be Deductible	No	No	Yes	Yes*
Can Medical Expenses On Owner And Family Be Set Up To Be Deductible	No	No	Yes	Yes*
Can Owner's Disability Insurance Be Set Up To Be Deductible	No	No	Yes	Yes*
Individual Retirement Accounts	Yes	Yes	Yes	Yes
Keough (H.R. 10) Plans	Yes	Yes	No	No
Qualified Pension And/Or Profit-Sharing Plans	No	No	Yes	Yes-with special restrictions
SEP (Simplified Employee Pension) Plans	Yes	Yes	Yes	Yes

Note: All the above items are subject to certain exceptions and restrictions.

*The Sub-Chapter S Tax Revision Act passed in late 1982 modified, and in many cases, eliminated these benefits. See your tax advisor for these changes as they pertain to your particular situation.

III. Payroll Taxes

A. The employer is **obligated by law** to pay the Internal Revenue Service 14.3% of the employee's first $42,000 of compensation as social security taxes. The employer has the right to collect (through a deduction from the payroll check) one-half of that amount from the employee. Treasury form #941 is used for the reporting and payment of this tax.

B. The employer **is obligated to withhold** federal income tax from his employees' wages. The employee **must sign** form W-4, which notifies the employer of how many exemptions are being claimed. Circular E is to be used in determining the amount of withholding. This employee tax is combined with the social security tax reported and paid with the utilization of forms #941.

C. All states have an **unemployment compensation law**. The tax to finance unemployment benefits is a tax on the employer. The states have various requirements, tax base amounts, and tax rates. Contact your local Employment Security Division to ascertain the requirements in your state.

D. The federal government also has an **unemployment tax** and you are subject to it if you are subject to the state unemployment tax. Generally speaking (and there are plenty of exceptions to this), the employer tax will be 1% of the first $7,000 of wages paid during the year. Reporting and payment requirements are fulfilled through the use of form #940. As with the State unemployment tax, this is a tax on you as an employer—you may not deduct it from the employees' paychecks.

E. Most states (and some counties and cities) have an **individual income tax** that must be withheld from the employees' wages. Contact your state and local departments of revenue for the details concerning payment and reporting.

F. Remember that any taxes withheld from an employee's salary **do not belong to you.** You are put in a fiduciary (or trust) position until they are remitted to the taxing authorities. The Internal Revenue Service is prone to deal harshly with the misuse of these funds. For this reason, many businesses maintain a separate checking account where they place the funds until time to remit to the taxing authorities. This procedure helps to assure that the funds are not used to cover operating expenses.

IV. Income Taxes

A. A proprietor/partner **will report the income** on his personal tax return (Form 1040). Generally, a shareholder in a Sub-Chapter S corporation also will report it on Form 1040.

B. Corporations pay **their own income tax** by filing Form 1120. The tax rate is 15% of the first $25,000, 18% of the next $25,000, 30% of the next $25,000, 40% of the next $25,000, and 46% of everything thereafter.

C. Most states have a personal income tax that closely conforms to the federal income tax in method of taxation. **The rates vary from state to state.**

D. Most states have a **corporate income tax**. Many times the tax bears little resemblance to the federal income tax method. (Some states call this a franchise tax.)

E. Other states have **varying forms of income taxation** under different names. (Unincorporated business tax and single business tax are examples of this.)

V. Other Taxes

A. Most localities have taxes on **personal property** and **real estate.** The law varies greatly. Equipment, inventories, and improvements to realty are the common items subject to personal property taxes.

B. Various state, county, and city permits, licenses, and registrations **sometimes** are required.

C. Most states have a **sales/use tax**. Although you will generally not be required to charge your patients this tax, you usually will have to pay it on many of your purchases.

D. According to the 1980 census, there are 39,471 jurisdictions (not including state and federal government) with various types of ordinances which might, depending upon their provisions, be applicable to their practice. These **laws** and **ordinances** are constantly being inacted, amended, or repealed. That is why it is vital to **seek professional advice** to avoid running afoul of the law.

VI. Depreciation

A. GENERAL RULE—There shall be allowed as a depreciation deduction a reasonable allowance for the exhaustion, wear and tear (including a reasonable allowance for obsolescence):
1. of property used in the trade or business, or
2. of property held for the production of income.
In the case of recovery property (within the meaning of section 168), the deduction allowable under section 168 shall be deemed to constitute the reasonable allowance provided by this section, except with respect to that portion of the basis of such property to which subsection (K) applies.
I.R.S. CODE SECTION 168(a) Allowance of deduction. There shall be allowed as a deduction for any taxable year the amount determined under this section with respect to recovery property."
I.R.S. CODE SECTION 168(c) Recovery property. For purposes of this title—(1) Recovery property defined. Except as provided in subsection (3), the term recovery property means tangible property of character subject to the allowance for depreciation (a) used in a trade or business, or (b) held for the production of income.

B. The 1981 Economic Recovery Tax Act (ERTA) introduced a new method for depreciation known as an "accelerated cost recovery system." (ACRS-pronounced acres). Technically the term depreciation, which most of us are somewhat familiar with, only applies to assets placed in service before January 1, 1981. This really is just a matter of semantics. All the cost recovery system amounts to is a somewhat rigid scale used to determine the amount of depreciation allowable in a particular year. The rates are generally based on an accelerated method (i.e. a larger deducation in the early years, a smaller one in the later years). In most cases, if the taxpayer so elects, straight-line rnethods over optional recovery periods may be used.

C. Under this system, all tangible assets are placed in categories known as recovery period categories. For instance, a business automobile would be placed in a three year category. Office equipment would be placed in a five year category. All this means is, that the car would be "written off" over a three year period and the office equipment over a five year period.

3 year category—3, 5, or 12 years
5 year category—5, 12, or 25 years
15 year category—15, 35, or 45 years
18 year category—18, 35, or 45 years
19 year category—19, 35, or 45 years

3 year/5 year WRITE OFF PERCENTAGES

	YEAR 1	YEAR 2	YEAR 3	YEAR 4	YEAR 5
3 YEAR PROPERTY	25%	38%	37%	-0-	-0-
5 YEAR PROPERTY	15%	22%	21%	21%	21%

It matters not what month 3 year and 5 year property was placed in service. The tax deduction for 3 year property in year 1 is 25% of the cost, regardless of what month during the year it was acquired. Thus, the tax deduction is the same for an asset placed in service in December as for an asset placed in service in January of the same year.

The month 15 year property is placed in service does matter.

15 YEAR WRITE OFF PERCENTAGES

MONTH PLACES IN SERVICE

YEAR	J	F	M	A	M	J	J	A	S	0	N	D
1	12	11	10	9	8	7	6	5	4	3	2	1
2	10	10	11	11	11	11	11	11	11	11	11	12
3	9	9	9	9	10	10	10	10	10	10	10	10
4	8	8	8	8	8	8	9	9	9	9	9	9
5	7	7	7	7	7	7	8	8	8	8	9	9
6	6	6	6	6	7	7	7	7	7	7	7	7
7	6	6	6	6	6	6	6	6	6	6	6	6
8	6	6	6	6	6	6	6	6	6	6	6	6
9	6	6	6	6	5	6	5	5	5	6	6	6
10	5	6	5	6	5	5	5	5	5	5	6	5
11	5	6	5	5	5	5	5	5	5	5	5	5
12	5	5	5	5	5	5	5	5	5	5	5	5
13	5	5	5	5	5	5	5	5	5	5	5	5
14	5	5	5	5	5	5	5	5	5	5	5	5
15	5	5	5	5	5	5	5	5	5	5	5	5
16	0	0	1	1	2	2	3	3	4	4	4	5

To illustrate, assume you established your home office in April. Your tax deduction for the first year would be 9% of the cost of the home office. The deduction for the second year would be 11%, the third year 9%, the fourth year 8%, and so on. As April was the month the office was originally established, you would merely match up the April column with the appropriate year to find the correct percentage.

VII. COST RECOVERY CATEGORIES

A. **3 year**—Automobiles, taxis, trucks weighing less than 13,000 pounds

B. **5 Year**—All equipment other than that included in the 3 and 15 year categories

C. **15 Year**—Real estate

D. To provide further examples of how ACRS works, assume the following: This year you purchase a $10,000 automobile and $800 of office equipment. By consulting the preceding charts, we find the tax deductions to be as follows:

YEAR	AUTO	Office Equip.
1	$ 2500	$120
2	3800	176
3	3700	168
4	-	168
5	-	168
6	-	-
7	-	-
8	-	-
9	-	-
10	-	-
11	-	-
12	-	-
13	-	-
14	-	-
15	-	-
Total	$10000	$800

E. **HOW TO HANDLE TRADE-INS:** One of the more troublesome areas of the average taxpayer is how to calculate the correct "basis" for an asset acquired by trade-in. this occurs most frequently in the area of automobiles. Many people erroneously assume that the dealer's list price is the cost of the auto and they compute depreciation from that amount.

F. Technically, when an asset is traded-in there is a gain or loss on the trade-in measured by the depreciation value against the trade-in allowance. However, this gain or loss goes "unrecognized" (i.e. it's not reportable on your tax return) if the asset is traded-in on another business asset.

G. To illustrate, assume that you acquire a $10,000 automobile that is 100% business, keep it two full years and then trade it in on another business automobile. The new car lists for $12,000, the dealer allows you $6000 on the old car and you give him a cash difference of $6000.

Cost of Auto #1			$10,000
ACRS Depreciation—Year #1	(25%)	$2500	
ACRS Depreciation—Year #2	(38%)	3800	(6,300)
Depreciated Value			$ 3,700
Dealer Trade-In Allowance			6,000
Gain (unrecognized)			$ 2,300
List Price—Auto #2			$12,000
Unrecognized Gain From Auto #1			(2,300)
Tax Basis—Auto #2			$ 9,700

Thus, the basis to be used to calculate depreciation for the second auto is $9,700, not the $12,000 list price. **This is because you had a "profit" of $2,300 on the trade-in but did not have to report it and pay tax on it.** The "profit" is deducted, in effect, from future depreciation allowances on auto #2. The reverse is also true. If you have a "loss" from a trade-in, that "loss" is added to the basis of the second car, therefore increasing future depreciation deductions.

H. **ELECTION TO EXPENSE:** One of the provisions of the Economic Recovery Tax Act is to allow a taxpayer to disregard depreciation and write-off in full up to a specified amount, the cost of recovery property classified as tangible personal property. The amount that may be treated in this manner is $5,000.

I. **STRAIGHT-LINE ACRS ELECTION:** You may elect ACRS percentages stated above and take straight-line deduction (i.e. an equal deduction in each year) over optional recovery periods.

VIII. INVESTMENT TAX CREDITS

A. The investment tax credit is available to all business persons holding "qualified property" used in their trade or business for the production of income. The tax reduction may, in some cases, completely eliminate the tax and may even result in a refund of tax paid in thje previous three years.

B. It is important to note that a tax credit is more valuable than a tax deduction. A tax credit results in a dollar-for-dollar reduction of income tax. A tax deduction returns no more than 50% of the deduction depending on your tax bracket. To illustrate, a $2,000 tax credit will save the full $2,000 in cash. A $2,000 tax deduction will save $1,000 to a taxpayer in the 50% tax bracket, $800 to a taxpayer in the 40% bracket, and so on.

C. The investment credit is allowed for the construction or purchase of equipment or other tangible depreciable property. Usually, real estate does not qualify for the investment credit. There are certain instances where real estate will qualify, but they are usually not applicable to situations. Examples of items that would normally qualify for the credit would include the business portion of an automobile, office equipment and furnishings, and therapy equipment.

D. The effect of the investment credit is as if the United States Treasury paid up to a specified percentage of the cost of the equipment. Thus, you are being "subsidized" to purchase business equipment. Hence, when the investment credit is combined with the cost recovery deduction allowances of the ACRS System explained in chapter 7, a substantial portion of the cost of the equipment can in effect be financed through tax savings.

E. For example, assume that you wish to purchase certain business equipment that costs $5,000. Also assume that you are in the 40% tax bracket.

		ACRS DEDUCTIONS	ACRS TAX SAVINGS	INVESTMENT CREDIT	TOTAL TAX SAVINGS
YEAR 1	(15%)	$ 750	$ 300	$500	$ 800
YEAR 2	(22%)	1,100	440	-	440
YEAR 3	(21%)	1,050	420	-	420
YEAR 4	(21%)	1,050	420	-	420
YEAR 5	(21%)	1,050	420	-	420
		$5,000	$2,000	$500	$2,500

ORIGINAL COST $5,000
TAX SAVINGS 2,500
NET COST $2,500

F. The investment tax credit is allowed for the year which the qualified property is **placed in service.** Thus, if equipment is purchased in year #1, but not put to a business use until year #2, the credit may be taken only in year #2. It matters not what month the property is placed in service during the year. Placing an asset in service in December yields the same credit as an asset placed in service in January. If you are contemplating the purchase of qualifying property, acquiring it in December of year #1 instead of January of year #2 would give you the credit (and therefore, the use of the money) nearly a full year earlier.

With a few exceptions, the amount of the credit is either 6% or 10% of the cost of the equipment.

1. **EQUIPMENT QUALIFYING FOR 6% CREDIT**
   Automobiles, taxis, trucks weighing less than 13,000 pounds.

2. **EQUIPMENT QUALIFYING FOR 10% CREDIT**
   All other tangible business property except real estate.

3. The investment credit is claimed by filing Form 3468 and attaching it to your tax return.

G. The Tax Equity and Fiscal Responsibility Act of 1982 modified the above schedule for assets placed in service after January 1, 1983. Basically the Act permits a choice of an 8% investment credit (4% on 3 year property) or a 10% credit with a downward basis adjustment for ACRS of one-half of the credit.

Form **3468**	**Computation of Investment Credit**	OMB No. 1545-0155
Department of the Treasury Internal Revenue Service (0)	► **Attach to your tax return.** ► **Schedule B (Business Energy Investment Credit) on back.**	**1985** 24

Name(s) as shown on return	Identifying number

Part I Elections (Check the box(es) below that apply to you (See Instruction D).)

A I elect to increase my qualified investment to 100% for certain commuter highway vehicles placed in service before January 1, 1986 (section 46(c)(6)) ☐

B I elect to increase my qualified investment by all qualified progress expenditures made this and all later tax years . . . . ☐
Enter total qualified progress expenditures included in column (4), Part II ► . . . .

C I claim full credit on certain ships under section 46(g)(3) (See **Instruction B** for details.) . . . . ☐

Part II Qualified Investment (See instructions for rules on automobiles and other property with any personal use)

1 Recovery Property			Line	**(1)** Class of Property	**(2)** Cost or Other Basis	**(3)** Applicable Percentage	**(4)** Qualified Investment (Column 2 x column 3)
Regular Percentage	New Property		(a)	3-year	*10 000*	60	*6 000*
			(b)	Other	*2 000*	100	*2 000*
	Used Property		(c)	3-year		60	
			(d)	Other		100	
Section 48(q) Election to Reduce Credit (instead of adjusting basis)	New Property		(e)	3-year		40	
			(f)	Other		80	
	Used Property		(g)	3-year		40	
			(h)	Other		80	

2	Nonrecovery property—Enter total qualified investment (See instructions for line 2)	2	
3	New commuter highway vehicle—Enter total qualified investment (See Instruction D(1))	3	
4	Used commuter highway vehicle—Enter total qualified investment (See Instruction D(1))	4	
5	Total qualified investment in 10% property—Add lines 1(a) through 1(h), 2, 3, and 4 (See instructions for special limits)	5	*8 000*
6	Qualified rehabilitation expenditures—Enter total qualified investment for:		
	a 30-year-old buildings	6a	
	b 40-year-old buildings	6b	
	c Certified historic structures (You must attach NPS certification—see instructions)	6c	

Part III Tentative Regular Investment Credit

7	10% of line 5	7	*800*
8	15% of line 6a	8	
9	20% of line 6b	9	
10	25% of line 6c	10	
11	Credit from cooperatives—Enter regular investment credit from cooperatives	11	
12	Regular investment credit—Add lines 7 through 11	12	*800*
13	Business energy investment credit—From line 11 of Schedule B (see back of this form)	13	
14	Current year investment credit—Add lines 12 and 13	14	*800*

Note: If you have a 1985 jobs credit (Form 5884), credit for alcohol used as fuel (Form 6478), or employee stock ownership plan (ESOP) credit (Form 8007) in addition to your 1985 investment credit, or if you have a carryback or carryforward of any general business credit, stop here and go to **Form 3800, General Business Credit,** to claim your 1985 investment credit. If you have only a 1985 investment credit (which may include business energy investment credit), you may continue with lines 15 through 20 to claim your credit.

Part IV Tax Liability Limitations

15	a Individuals—From Form 1040, enter amount from line 46 . . . . }	15	
	b Corporations—From Form 1120, Schedule J, enter tax from line 3 (or Form 1120-A, Part I, line 1). . .		
	c Other filers —Enter income tax before credits from return . . . . }		
16	a Individuals—From Form 1040, enter credit from line 47, plus any orphan drug, nonconventional source fuel, and research credits included on line 49 }		
	b Corporations—From Form 1120, Schedule J, enter credits from lines 4(a) through 4(e) (Form 1120-A filers, enter zero) . . . . } . .	16	
	c Other filers—See instructions for line 16c . . . . }		
17	Income tax liability as adjusted (subtract line 16 from line 15).	17	
18	a Enter smaller of line 17 or $25,000. (See instructions for line 18)	18a	
	b If line 17 is more than $25,000—Enter 85% of the excess.	18b	
19	Investment credit limitation—Add lines 18a and 18b	19	
20	Total allowed credit—Enter the smaller of line 14 or line 19. This is your **General Business Credit** for 1985. Enter here and on Form 1040, line 48; Form 1120, Schedule J, line 4(f); Form 1120-A, Part I, line 2 ; or the proper line of other returns	20	

For Paperwork Reduction Act Notice, see separate instructions.   Form **3468** (1985)

H. It is important to note that all or part of the investment credit may be "recaptured" (i.e. paid back). The investment credit is considered a "tentative" credit. The credit is allowed in the year the property is placed in service, but only "earned" by holding the property a specified number of years. If you acquire property qualifying for the 10% credit in year #1, but dispose of that property in year #2, you have not "earned" the credit, and therefore must pay it back. In such a case, Form 4255 must be completed to calculate the repayment.

(5) SPECIAL RULES FOR RECOVERY PROPERTY—
    (a) GENERAL RULE—If, during any taxable year, section 38 recovery property is disposed of, or otherwise ceases to be section 38 property with respect to the taxpayer before the close of the recapture period, then, except as provided in subparagraph (D), the tax under this chapter for such taxable year shall be increased by the recapture percentage of the aggregate decrease in the credits allowed under section 38 for all prior taxable years which would have resulted solely from reducing to zero the qualified investment taken into account with respect to such property.

    (B) RECAPTURE PERCENTAGE—For purposes of subparagraph (A), the recapture percentage shall be determined in accordance with the following table:

If the recovery property ceases to be section 38 property within—	The recapture percentage is:	
	For 15-year, 10-year, and 5-year property	For 3-year property
One full year after placed in service	10	100
One full year after the close of the period described in clause (i)	80	66
One full year after the close of the period described in clause (ii)	60	33
One full year after the close of the period described in clause (iii)	40	0
One full year after the close of the period described in clause (iv)	20	0

SECTION 47
SEC. 47. CERTAIN DISPOSITIONS, ETC., OF SECTION 38 PROPERTY

SECTION 47(a)

(1) (a) GENERAL RULE—Under regulations prescribed by the Secretary—
    (1) EARLY DISPOSITION, ETC.—If during any taxable year any property is disposed of, or otherwise ceases to be section 38 property with respect to the taxpayer, before the close of the useful life which was taken into account in computing the credit under section 38, then the tax under this chapter for such taxable year shall be increased by an amount equal to the aggregate decrease in the credits allowed under section 38 for all prior taxable years which would have resulted solely from substituting, in determining qualified investment, for such useful life the period beginning with the time such property was placed in service by the taxpayer and ending with the time such property ceased to be section 38 property.

-220-

Form **4255**
(Rev. September 1985)
Department of the Treasury
Internal Revenue Service

Recapture of Investment Credit
(Including Energy Investment Credit)
▶ Attach to your income tax return.

OMB No. 1545-0166
Expires 8-31-88

65

Name(s) as shown on return

Identifying number

Properties	Kind of property—State whether recovery or nonrecovery (see the Instructions for Form 3468 for definitions). If energy property, show type. Also indicate if rehabilitation expenditure property.
A	*Business Automobile*
B	
C	
D	
E	

Computation Steps: (see Specific Instructions)

Original Investment Credit

		A	B	C	D	E
1	Original rate of credit	10 %				
2	Date property was placed in service	12-1-84				
3	Cost or other basis	10 000				
4	Original estimated useful life or class of property	3 YR				
5	Applicable percentage	60 %				
6	Original qualified investment (line 3 times line 5)	6000				
7	Original credit (line 1 times line 6)	600				
8	Date property ceased to be qualified investment credit property	11-7-85				
9	Number of full years between the date on line 2 and the date on line 8	0				

Computation of Recapture Tax

		A	B	C	D	E
10	Recapture percentage (from instructions)	100 %				
11	Tentative recapture tax (line 7 times line 10)	600				

12 Add line 11, columns A through E 600

13 Enter tax from property ceasing to be at risk, or for which there was an increase in nonqualified nonrecourse financing (attach separate computation) . . . .

14 Total—Add lines 12 and 13 600

15 Portion of original credit (line 7) not used to offset tax in any year, **plus** any carryback and carryforward of credits you can now apply to the original credit year because you have freed up tax liability in the amount of the tax recaptured (Do not enter more than line 14—see instructions) . . . .

16 Total increase in tax—Subtract line 15 from line 14. Enter here and on the proper line of your tax return. 600

General Instructions

(Section references are to the Internal Revenue Code, unless otherwise noted.)

Paperwork Reduction Act Notice.—We ask for this information to carry out the Internal Revenue laws of the United States. We need it to ensure that taxpayers are complying with these laws and to allow us to figure and collect the right amount of tax. You are required to give us this information.

Purpose of Form.—Use Form 4255 to figure the increase in tax for the recapture of investment credit and energy property. You must refigure the credit if you took it in an earlier year, but disposed of the property before the end of the recapture period or the useful life you used to figure the original credit. You must also refigure the credit if you changed the use of the property so that it no longer qualifies as regular or energy investment credit property. For example, you

must refigure the credit if you change the use of property from business use to personal use, or if there is any decrease in the percentage of business use of investment credit property. See sections 47(a)(3) and 47(a)(5)(C) for information on recapture for progress expenditure property. Also, see the instructions for line 13 regarding recapture if property ceases to be at risk, or if there is an increase in nonqualified, nonrecourse financing related to certain at-risk property placed in service after July 18, 1984.

IX. HOME OFFICE

A. The cost or maintaining an office in the home is deductible if it is used "exclusively and on a regular basis as your principal place of business or a place of business that is used by customers in meeting or dealing with you in the normal course of your business."

SECTION 280A
SEC. 280A. DISALLOWANCE OF CERTAIN EXPENSES IN CONNECTION WITH BUSINESS USE OF HOME, RENTAL OR VACATION HOMES, ETC.

Sec. 280A(a)

(a) GENERAL RULE—Except as otherwise provided in this section, in the case of a taxpayer who is an individual or an electing small business corporation, no deduction otherwise allowable under this chapter shall be allowed with respect to the use of a dwelling unit which is used by taxpayer during the taxable year as a residence.

Sec. 280A(c)

(c) EXCEPTIONS FOR CERTAIN BUSINESS OR RENTAL USE; LIMITATION ON DEDUCTIONS FOR SUCH USE.

(1) CERTAIN BUSINESS USE—Subsection (a) shall not apply to any item to the extent such item is allocable to a portion of the dwelling unit which is exclusively used on a regular basis—

    (a) (as) the principal place of business for any trade or business of the taxpayer,

    (B) as a place of business which is used by patients, clients, or customers in meeting or dealing with the taxpayer in the normal course of his trade or business, or

    (C) in the case of a separate structure which is not attached to the dwelling unit, in connection with the taxpayer's trade or business.

In the case of an employee, the preceding sentence shall apply only if the exclusive use referred to in the preceding sentence is for the convenience of his employer.

(2) CERTAIN STORAGE USE—Subsection (a) shall not apply to any item to the extent such item is allocable to space within the dwelling unit which is used on a regular basis as a storage unit for the inventory of the taxpayer held for use in the taxpayer's trade or business or selling products at retail or wholesale, but only if the dwelling unit is the sole fixed location of such trade or business.

B. Taxpayers who carry on a "second" business may deduct home office expenses where the office in the home is the principal place of business, for the second business. An occasional or incidental business use of the space does not qualify as deductible.

C. **LIMITATION:** The home office deduction may not exceed the gross income from the business less allocated mortgage interest and real estate taxes. For example:

Gross income	$6,000
Less home office portion of mortgage interest and taxes	2,000
Remaining home office expenses may not exceed	$4,000

D. **COMPUTING THE HOME OFFICE DEDUCTION:** All expenses of maintaining the home office that can be identified are deductible. This includes depreciation, furnishings, mortgage interest, utilities, insurance, real estate taxes and repairs and maintenance.

The first step is to calculate the square footage used as an office and the total square footage of the home. Exclude the garage from this computation.

EXAMPLE

Home office	400 sq. ft.	20%
Home	2000 sq. ft.	100%

Therefore 20% of the expenses qualify as a deductible item. To compute allowable depreciation, make the following computations to discover the basis for depreciation of the home office.

A. Lower of original cost of home or market value on date put into business use.		$80,000
B. Less-estimated cost of land	$8,000	
C. Less-estimated cost of garage	8,000	16,000
D. Equals-net basis of home		$64,000
E. Home office percentage		20%
F. Equals-basis of home office		$12,800

$12,800 is the basis to be used in computing depreciation. All other expenses allowable are deductible on the percentage basis (in the example, 20% of interest 20% of insurance, etc). Expenses incurred directly for the home office portion only. Generally, costs of maintaining the exterior such as lawnmowing and landscaping are not dedectible at all. Unless you can establish a business need for the services, the cost of water and refuse removal should not be included as a business expense.

E. **A WARNING:** Although the home office deduction affords a tax-shelter of sorts, it can come back to haunt you if you sell the residence. The Internal Revenue Code permits a taxpayer to defer reporting the gain from the sale of a residence if within 24 months the taxpayer buys another residence at a cost in excess of the selling price of the first residence. The Code also permits a once-in-a-lifetime opportunity for taxpayers to escape taxes completely on a gain of up to $125,000 after age 55. In the normal situation, most taxpayers will never pay tax on the sale of their residence. In their younger years, they normally do replace each residence they sell with a more expensive one and then in their later years trade down to a more inexpensive one. Thus the two methods of avoiding taxes on the sale of the residence serve their purpose.

But these exclusions are for *personal residences only*. They do not apply to business property, and the home office is considered business property. It is quite possible that as inflation pushes up the value of a residence, the capital gains tax to be paid on the sale of the home office portion of the house would far exceed the depreciation deduction allowed in previous years.

Assume a home with a cost of $40,000 and a home office basis of $10,000. Further assume that over the years, depreciation deductions of $1,000 have been taken. Inflation pushes the house's value up to $100,000 and you sell. The following allocation must be made.

	Total	Personal	Business
Cost	$ 40,000	$30,000	$10,000
Less-Depreciation	(1,000)	-0-	(1,000)
Tax Basis	$ 39,000	$30,000	$ 9,000
%	100.00%	76.9%	23.1%
Allocated Selling Price	$100,000	$76,900	$23,100
Gain	$ 71,000	$46,900	$14,100

The $14,000 gain would be subject to a capital gains tax. The maximum capital gains tax is 20% of the gain. For this purpose, assume you are in a 40% bracket.

Capital Gain	$14,100
60% excluded by law	8,460
Taxable	5,640
@ 40% tax bracket	°40%
TAX	$ 2,256

The savings realized from depreciation on the property was $400 ($100 depreciation x 40% tax bracket). It therefore **costs money** to claim the home office deduction under these circumstances.

(Sec. 274)
SEC. 274, DISALLOWANCE OF CERTAIN ENTERTAINMENT, ETC., EXPENSES.

(Sec. 274(a))
ENTERTAINMENT, AMUSEMENT, OR RECREATION—

(1) IN GENERAL—No deduction otherwise allowable under this chapter shall be allowed for any item—
  (A) ACTIVITY—With respect to an activity which is of a type generally considered to constitute entertainment, amusement, or recreation, unless the taxpayer establishes that the item was directly related to, or, in the case of an item directly preceding or following a substantial and bona fide business discussion (including business meetings at a convention or otherwise), that such item was associated with, the active conduct of the taxpayer's trade or business, or
  (B) FACILITY—With respect to a facility used in connection with an activity referred to in subparagraph (A).
In the case of an item described in subparagraph (A), the deduction shall in no event exceed the portion of such item which meets the requirements of subparagraph (A).

(2) SPECIAL RULES—For purposes of applying paragraph (1)—
  (A) Dues or fees to any social, athletic, or sporting club or organization shall be treated as items with respect to facilities.
  (B) An activity described in section 212 shall be treated as a trade or business.
  (C) In the case of a club, paragraph (1)(B) shall apply unless the taxpayer establishes that the facility was used primarily for the furtherance of the taxpayer's trade or business and that the item was directly related to the active conduct of such trade or business.

(Sec. 274(d))

(d) SUBSTANTIATION REQUIRED—No deduction shall be allowed—
  (1) under section 162 or 212 for any traveling expense (including meals and lodging while away from home),
  (2) for any item with respect to an activity which is of a type generally considered to constitute entertainment, amusement, or recreation, or with respect to a facility used in connection with such an activity, or
(3) for any expense for gifts,
unless the taxpayer substantiates by adequate records or by sufficient evidence corroborating his own statement (A) the amount of such expense or other item, (B) the time and place of the travel, entertainment, amusement, recreation, or use of the facility, or the date and description of the gift, (C) the business purpose of the expense or other item, and (D) the business relationship to the taxpayer of persons entertained, using the facility, or receiving the gift. The Secretary may by regulations provide that some or all of the requirements of the preceding sentence shall not apply in the case of an expense which does not exceed an amount prescribed pursuant to such regulations.

(Sec. 274(e))

(e) SPECIFIC EXCEPTIONS TO APPLICATION OF SUBSECTION (a)—shall not apply to—
  (1) BUSINESS MEALS—Expenses for food and beverages furnished to any individual under circumstances which (taking into account the surroundings in which furnished, the taxpayer's trade, business, or income-producing activity and the relationship to such trade, business, or activity of the persons to whom the food and beverages are furnished) are of a type generally considered to be conducive to a business discussion.

A. **ENTERTAINMENT:** Because of the nature of the business, most clinicians incur entertainment expenses in the normal course of their activities. These will include social functions, special events, meals and other forms of entertainment. A tax deduction will be allowed if it can be shown that the expenditure was either "associated with or directly related to" the conduct of your business activities. Even if the expenditures do not result in business income, they are still deductible. I.R.S. regulations list the following requirements for a deductible entertainment expense:

1. There must be a present or future potential for income.
2. There was an active participation in a meeting negotiation, or discussion during the entertainment period.
3. The main purpose of the combined business and entertainment was business.

The Internal Revnue Act of 1978 disallowed expenses for most "entertainment facilities." The Act excluded Country Clubs from the category of entertainment facilities. However, the Act only affected the **cost of the facility** and not the actual entertainment expense incurred at the facility. For instance, dues to the Country Club will be deductible if it can be proven that the primary use of the Club is for business purposes. If it can be established, for example, that 75% of the activities you engage in at the Club are business related, then 75% of the dues are deductible.

The "entertainment facilities" rule does not affect other entertainment expenses, such as business meals. The meals for the business contact, the clinician, and even their spouses will be deductible if the Internal Revenue Service can be shown that the expenses meet the tests of "ordinary and necessary", given the nature of the taxpayer's business.

B. **TRAVEL:** Expenses incurred while "away from home" for business are deductible. Travel expenses are distinguished from local transportation costs by the Internal Revenue Service. Local Transportation costs are those costs incurred while going from client to client and **not incurred while away from home.** All business transporation costs are deductible (cabs, trains, automobiles, airplanes, etc.).

The expenses of going from home to the office are called commuting expenses. They are not deductible. The Internal Revenue Service will disallow the cost of going from home to the first business stop of the day. All subsequent stops are deductible. But if the clinician first stops at the office before making the first call of the day, then the expenses between the office and the first client will be allowed. However, if your office is in your home, then it is impossible to have commuting expenses. Then, the costs incurred between home and the first client would be deductible.

C. **AWAY FROM HOME:** For travel expenses to be deductible, they must be incurred while "away from home" on business. Your tax home is located at (1) principal place of business, or (2) if the taxpayer has no principal place of business, then at the regular place of abode.

If a taxpayer cannot qualify in either of the above categories, then he/she is considered an itinerant who has home wherever he/she happens to be working, and thus is never "away from home" for purposes of the tax deduction for traveling expenses.

D. **BUSINESS GIFTS:** The deduction for business gifts is limited to $25 per recipient per year. Items clearly of an advertising nature costing less than $4 are not included in the limitation.

(Sec. 274(b))

(b) GIFTS—

    (1) LIMITATION—No deduction shall be allowed under section 162 or section 212 for any expense for gifts made directly or indirectly to any individual to the extent that such expense, when added to prior expenses of the taxpayer for gifts made to such individual during the same taxable year, exceeds $25. For purposes of this section, the term "gift" means any item excludable from gross income of the recipient under section 102 which is not excludable from his gross income under any other provision of this chapter, but such term does not include—

        (A) An item having a cost to the taxpayer not in excess of $4.00 on which the one of a number of identical items distributed generally by the taxpayer,

        (B) a sign, display rack, or other promotional material to be used on the business premises of the recipient, or

        (C) an item of tangible personal property which is awarded to an employee by reason of length of service, productivity, or safety achievement, but only to the extent that—

            (i) the cost of such item to the taxpayer does not exceed $400, or

            (ii) such items is a qualified plan award.

XI. AUTOMOBILE EXPENSES

A. Automobile expenses are incurred by most taxpayers as a necessity in their practice. The law permits tax deductions for these expenses. It does not matter if the taxpayer is self-employed or its employed by others. If the automobile is used for business purposes, tax deductions may be claimed.

There are two methods for determining the deductible automobile expenses, known as the optional method and the actual method.

B. **OPTIONAL METHOD:** This method provides for a stated per-mile rate for business use. For 1986, the rate is 21¢ per mile. In addition, once a car accumulates 60,000 on it, it is considered fully depreciated. All miles over 60,000 qualify only for 11¢ per mile.

The optional method is available only to taxpayers who own their car. It is not available to those who lease. Using this method, it is necessary only to keep a log of business miles. Record keeping is therefore kept to a minimum and many individuals use this method for that reason only. However, since this per-mile rate is in lieu of depreciation, gas, oil, tires, insurance and operating costs, it may result in an understatement of the true costs of operating the business vehicle.

In addition to the per-mile deduction, you are permitted to deduct interest, parking, fees, tolls and sales tax.

C. **ACTUAL METHOD:** This method permits you to deduct the actual operating costs plus depreciation. Unlike the Optional Method, where the record-keeping is relatively simple, a greater amount of detail is necessary.

D. In addition to the mileage log required under the Optional Method, receipts must be kept for gas, oil, repairs and other operating costs. The odemeter must be read each January 1 to determine the total mileage put on the car each year. The log will reflect the business miles and the operating costs must be pro-rated between personal and business.

For example, assume that the mileage log reflects business mileage of 17,347 and the odemeter shows that a **total** of 27,250 miles were driven during the year. Further assume that the actual operating costs were as follows:

Gasoline and oil	$1908
Repairs	625
Tires, supplies	350
Insurance	500
Taxes	300
Interest	800
Sub-Total	4583
Parking/Tolls	150
	4733

The deduction under the Optional Method would be:

17,347 miles	@	21¢	$3643
Interest $800	@63.66%		509
Parking/tolls			150
State Ex. $300	@63.66%		191
			$4493

The deduction under the Actual Method would be:

Business miles	17,347	63.66%
Personal miles	9,903	36.34
Total miles	27,250	100.00%

63.66% of $4583 + $150 parking and tolls + depreciation (in the example $2500) = $5568.

It should be noted that the interest, any sales tax, and depending on your states license tax system, the license tax not permitted as a business expense qualify as itemized deduction on Schedule A of your tax return. (In the example, 36.34% of the interest and the state excise tax).

SCHEDULE C
(Form 1040)

Department of the Treasury
Internal Revenue Service (O)

Profit or (Loss) From Business or Profession
(Sole Proprietorship)

Partnerships, Joint Ventures, etc., Must File Form 1065.

▶ Attach to Form 1040 or Form 1041.   ▶ See Instructions for Schedule C (Form 1040).

OMB No. 1545-0074

1985
09

Name of proprietor	Social security number

A Principal business or profession, including product or service (see Instructions) | **B** Principal business code from page 2

C Business name and address ▶ .... | **D** Employer ID number

E Method(s) used to value closing inventory:
(1) ☐ Cost   (2) ☐ Lower of cost or market   (3) ☐ Other (attach explanation)

F Accounting method: (1) ☐ Cash   (2) ☐ Accrual   (3) ☐ Other (specify) ▶ ....

	Yes	No
G Was there any change in determining quantities, costs, or valuations between opening and closing inventory?.		
If "Yes," attach explanation.		
H Did you deduct expenses for an office in your home?		

Part I   Income

1 a Gross receipts or sales	1a	
b Less: Returns and allowances	1b	
c Subtract line 1b from line 1a and enter the balance here	1c	
2 Cost of goods sold and/or operations (from Part III, line 8)	2	
3 Subtract line 2 from line 1c and enter the **gross profit** here.	3	
4 a Windfall Profit Tax Credit or Refund received in 1985 (see Instructions)	4a	
b Other income	4b	
5 Add lines 3, 4a, and 4b. This is the **gross income** . . . . ▶	5	

Part II   Deductions

6 Advertising			**22** Pension and profit-sharing plans . .		
7 Bad debts from sales or services (Cash method taxpayers, see Instructions)			**23** Rent on business property		
			24 Repairs		
8 Bank service charges			**25** Supplies (not included in Part III below)		
9 Car and truck expenses			**26** Taxes (Do not include Windfall Profit Tax here. See line 30. **63.66%**		**191**
10 Commissions					
11 Depletion			**27** Travel and entertainment		
12 Depreciation and section 179 deduction from Form 4562 (not included in Part III below)			**28** Utilities and telephone		
			29 a Wages . .		
			b Jobs credit .		
13 Dues and publications			**c** Subtract line 29b from 29a . .		
14 Employee benefit programs . . .			**30** Windfall Profit Tax withheld in 1985		
15 Freight (not included in Part III below) .			**31** Other expenses (specify):		
16 Insurance			**a** *17347 MILES @ 21¢*		*3643*
17 Laundry and cleaning			**b** *PARKING / TOLLS*		*150*
18 Legal and professional services . .			**c**		
19 Mortgage interest paid to financial institutions (see Instructions)			**d**		
			e		
20 Office expense			**f**		
21 Other interest **63.66 %** . .		**509**	**g**		
32 Add amounts in columns for lines 6 through 31g. These are the **total deductions** . . . . ▶				32	

33 Net profit or (loss). Subtract line 32 from line 5 and enter the result. If a profit, enter on Form 1040, line 12, and on Schedule SE, Part I, line 2 (or Form 1041, line 5). If a loss, you MUST go on to line 34 . . . . . . | 33

34 If you have a loss, you **MUST** answer this question: "Do you have amounts for which you are not at risk in this business (see Instructions)?" ☐ Yes ☐ No
If "Yes," you MUST attach **Form 6198.** If "No," enter the loss on Form 1040, line 12; and on Schedule SE, Part I, line 2 (or Form 1041, line 5).

Part III   Cost of Goods Sold and/or Operations (See Schedule C Instructions for Part III)

1 Inventory at beginning of year (if different from last year's closing inventory, attach explanation)	1	
2 Purchases less cost of items withdrawn for personal use	2	
3 Cost of labor (do not include salary paid to yourself)	3	
4 Materials and supplies	4	
5 Other costs	5	
6 Add lines 1 through 5	6	
7 Less: Inventory at end of year	7	
8 Cost of goods sold and/or operations. Subtract line 7 from line 6. Enter here and in Part I, line 2, above. . .	8	

For Paperwork Reduction Act Notice, see Form 1040 Instructions.

Schedule C (Form 1040) 1985

Form **2106**	**Employee Business Expenses**	OMB No. 1545-0139
Department of the Treasury Internal Revenue Service (O)	▶ See instructions on back. ▶ Attach to Form 1040.	**1985** 54

Your name	Social security number	Occupation in which expenses were incurred
	: :	

Part I Employee Business Expenses Deductible in Figuring Adjusted Gross Income

1 Vehicle expenses from Part II, lines 15 or 22	1	5 418
2 Parking fees, tolls, and certain other expenses (see instructions)	2	150
3 Local transportation including train, cabs, bus, airplane, etc.	3	
4 Travel expenses while away from home overnight including meals, lodging, airplane, car rental, taxi, etc.	4	
5 Employees who are not outside salespersons: Enter your expenses, not included on lines 1 through 4, for entertainment, gifts, and other business expenses, up to the amount you were reimbursed by your employer. Use Schedule A (Form 1040) for these expenses that were more than your reimbursement	5	
6 Outside salesperson's expenses: Enter your total expenses for entertainment, gifts, and other business expenses not included on lines 1 through 4	6	
7 Add lines 1 through 6	7	5 568
8 Enter reimbursements from employer on this line if the reimbursements were not included on Form W-2	8	
9 If line 7 is more than line 8, enter difference here and on Form 1040, line 25	9	5 568
10 If line 8 is more than line 7, enter difference here and include it on Form 1040, line 7	10	

Part II Vehicle Expenses (Use either your actual expenses or the standard mileage rate.)

Section A.—General Information

		Vehicle 1	Vehicle 2
1 Enter the date vehicle was placed in service	1	/ /	/ /
2 Total mileage vehicle was used during 1985	2	27 250 miles	miles
3 Miles included on line 2 that vehicle was used for business	3	17 347 miles	miles
4 Percent of business use (divide line 3 by line 2)	4	63.66 %	%
5 Average daily round trip commuting distance	5	10 miles	miles
6 Miles included on line 2 that vehicle was used for commuting	6	2500 miles	miles
7 Other personal mileage (subtract line 6 plus line 3 from line 2)	7	7403 miles	miles

8 Do you (or your spouse) have another vehicle available for personal purposes? ☒ Yes ☐ No
9 If your employer provided you with a vehicle, is personal use during off duty hours permitted? ☐ Yes ☐ No ☒ Not applicable
10 Do you have evidence to support your deduction? ☒ Yes ☐ No. If yes, is the evidence written? ☒ Yes ☐ No

Section B.—Standard Mileage Rate (Do not use this section unless you own the vehicle)

11 Enter the smaller of Part II, line 3 or 15,000 miles	11	miles
12 Subtract line 11 from Part II, line 3	12	miles
13 Multiply line 11 by 21¢ (.21) (see instructions for a fully depreciated vehicle)	13	
14 Multiply line 12 by 11¢ (.11)	14	
15 Add lines 13 and 14. Enter total here and on Part I, line 1	15	

Section C.—Actual Expenses

		Vehicle 1	Vehicle 2
16 Gasoline, oil, repairs, vehicle insurance, etc.	16	4 583	
17 Vehicle rentals	17		
18 Value of employer-provided vehicle (applies only if included on Form W-2 at 100% fair rental value, see instructions)	18		
19 Add lines 16 through 18	19	4 583	
20 Multiply line 19 by the percentage on Part II, line 4	20	2 918	
21 Depreciation from Section D, column (f) (see instructions)	21	2 500	
22 Add lines 20 and 21. Enter total here and on Part I, line 1	22	5 418	

Section D.—Depreciation of Vehicles (Depreciation can only be claimed for a vehicle you own. If a vehicle is used 50 percent or less in a trade or business, the Section 179 deduction is not allowed and depreciation must be taken using the straight line method. For other limitations, see instructions.)

	Cost or other basis (a)	Basis for depreciation (Business use only—see instructions) (b)	Method of figuring depreciation (c)	Depreciation deduction (d)	Section 179 expense (e)	Total column (d) + column (e) (f)
Vehicle 1	15 708	10 000	PRE	2 500	0	2 500
Vehicle 2						

For Paperwork Reduction Act Notice, see Instructions.   Form **2106** (1985)

XII. RETIREMENT PLANS

A. Several options and opportunities for the clinician exist to tax-shelter significant amounts of money through the use of a tax-deferred retirement plan.

INDIVIDUAL RETIREMENT ACCOUNT (IRA)

(a) ALLOWANCE OF DEDUCTION—In the case of an individual, there shall be allowed as a deduction an amount equal to the qualified retirement contributions of the individual for the taxable year.

(Sec. 219(b))

(b) MAXIMUM AMOUNT OF DEDUCTION—
(1) IN GENERAL—The amount allowable as a deduction under subsection (a) to any individual for any taxable year shall not exceed the lesser of—
(A) $2,000, or
(B) an amount equal to the compensation includible in the individual's gross income for such taxable year.

B. All employees and self-employed persons who receive compensation are eligible for an IRA plan, even if they are covered under other retirement plans. The amount of the contribution to the plan is the lesser of (a) $2,000 or (b) 100% of earnings. Earnings for the self-employed individuals equals that amount after all business expenses reflected at the bottom of Schedule C.

C. There are many institutions offering IRA plans. They are not all the same and the taxpayer should compare the various plans before investing. However, you are not "locked in" to a particular plan. If you find that you prefer to change, for whatever reason, the regulations permit you to "rollover" the IRA to a different institution once a year.

The only restrictions on the "roll over" are (1) the funds from the first IRA must be placed in the second IRA within 60 days of distribution from the first plan and (2) If property other than money is distributed from the first plan, that same property must be placed in the second IRA.

These are a number of places to invest in an IRA. These include:

Commerical Banks
Savings and Loan Associations
Insurance Companies
Credit Unions
Money Markets
Stock and Bonds

D. **AFTER-TAX COST:** As the investment in a retirement plan is tax deductible, the true cost is somewhat less than the contribution:

AFTER-TAX COST (BRACKET)

contribution	(50%)	(44%)	(33%)	(25%)	(19%)
$ 2,000	$1,000	$1,120	$1,340	$1,500	$1,620
3,000	1,500	1,680	2,010	2,250	2,430
5,000	2,500	2,800	3,350	3,750	4,050
10,000	-5,000	5,600	6,700	7,500	8,100
15,000	7,500	8,400	10,050	11,250	12,150

It must be remembered that these plans are tax-**deferred** plans. Upon distribution from the plan, these proceeds are taxable. The real gain comes from the facts (a) that as the plan's earnings are not taxable, the plan will grow at a faster rate, and (b) most individuals will be in a lower tax bracket during their retirement years than during their working years.

E. **KEOUGH PLANS:** If you are in a position where you would like to contribute more than $2,000 to a retirement plan, a Keough (sometimes called HR-100) plan may be established. Keough plans are only available to self-employed individuals.

The limitation is the lesser of (a) 20% of earned income or (b) $30,000. For example, an individual earning $30,000 per year can contribute $6,000 (20%) to a Keough Plan. In addition to the Keough Plan, an individual can establish an IRA and contribute an additional $2,000 for a total of $8,000 in tax-deferred retirement plans.

The distribution rules for a Keough Plan are much the same as the rules discussed earlier for IRA's.

A self-employed individual who institutes a Keough Plan must also include, on a non-discriminatory basis, all employees with three or more years of service. Seasonal and part-time employees can be excluded.

A Keough Plan may be funded by:
1 cash contributions to a trust or custodial account held by a commercial bank, savings and loan association or Federal credit union—
2 cash purchases of an annuity, endowment or life insurance contract issued by a life insurance company.
3 cash purchase from an investment company of face amount certificates.
4 cash investments in mutual funds accounts where the funds are used to purchase stocks, bonds or money market instruments.

It is amazing to see what the magic of compounding will do with money left in an IRA. Assuming a $2,000 annual contribution and an interest rate of 12% the plan will be worth:

```
Year 10  $    31,756
Year 20  $   143,211
Year 30  $   610,372
Year 40  $1,645,250
```

An individual, age 25, would have $1,645,250 in the IRA by age 65!

If your spouse works (either with you or elsewhere) he/she would also be eligible to establish an IRA plan. This would double the amounts reflected above. If your spouse does not work, you are permitted to establish a "Spousal IRA" and contribute up to $2,250 to it.

One of the significant things about the IRA plans is that the deduction is taken from gross income. It is always allowed. Therefore, even people who do not itemize their deductions will still receive the tax deduction.

The earnings on an IRA are exempt from tax until distributed. This allows the fund to grow at a much faster rate than if it were taxed.

F. **DISTRIBUTIONS:** To encourage individuals to use the IRA plan for its intended purpose, i.e. a retirement plan, the Internal Revenue Service imposes a 10% penalty tax on any distributions before age 59½. This penalty is in addition to the regular tax that would be due. The only exceptions are in the case of disability or death.

Distributions from the plan should commence between ages 59½ and 70½. If distributions do not start by age 70½, a severe penalty tax is imposed. Using life expectancy tables for a person age 70½, the IRS computes a "minimum distribution" (the amount that should be distributed each year to fully distribute the account over the the life expectancy.) If the amount actually distributed is less than this "minimum distribution," a penalty of 50% of the difference may be levied.

FEEDBACK

To: Donald E. Hendrickson, Ed.D., P.C.
Psychologist Associates
2810 Ethel Avenue
Suite 2
Muncie, IN 47304

The parts of How to Establish Your Own Independent Private Practice, that I have found most helpful are (please note pages and reasons, if appropriate):

I would find the book more useful if you would elaborate on the following (please note pages and reasons, if appropriate):

Other Comments:

Name: _____

Organization: _____

Street: _____

City: _____

State: _____ ZIP: _____